Sir Noël Coward

His Words And Music

A COLLECTION OF 32 COWARD CLASSICS

CHAPPELL & CO., INC.

RANDOM HOUSE
NEW YORK

Exclusive Distributor to the Book Trade

ISBN 0-394-70978-0
Library of Congress Catalog Card Number 73-1154

INTRODUCTION
by Sir Noël Coward

I was born into a generation that still took light music seriously. The lyrics and melodies of Gilbert and Sullivan were hummed and strummed into my consciousness at an early age. My father sang them, my mother played them, my nurse, Emma, breathed them through her teeth while she was washing me, dressing me and undressing me and putting me to bed. My aunts and uncles, who were legion, sang them singly and in unison at the slightest provocation. By the time I was four years old 'Take a Pair of Sparkling Eyes', 'Tit Willow', 'We're Very Wide Awake, the Moon and I' and 'I Have a Song to Sing-O' had been fairly inculcated into my bloodstream.

The whole Edwardian era was saturated with operetta and musical comedy: in addition to popular foreign importations by Franz Lehar, Leo Fall, André Messager, etc., our own native composers were writing musical scores of a quality that has never been equalled in this country since the 1914-18 war. Lionel Monckton, Paul Rubens, Ivan Caryll and Leslie Stuart were flourishing. 'The Quaker Girl',

'Our Miss Gibbs', 'Miss Hook of Holland', 'Florodora', 'The Arcadians' and 'The Country Girl', to name only a few, were all fine musical achievements, and over and above the artists who performed them, the librettists who wrote them and the impresarios who presented them, their music was the basis of their success. Their famous and easily remembered melodies can still be heard on the radio and elsewhere, but it was in the completeness of their scores that their real strength lay: opening choruses, finales, trios, quartettes and concerted numbers — all musicianly, all well balanced and all beautifully constructed.

There was no song-plugging in those days beyond an occasional reprise in the last act; there was no assaulting of the ear by monstrous repetition, no unmannerly nagging. A little while ago I went to an American 'musical' in which the hit number was reprised no less than five times during the performance by different members of the cast, as well as being used in the overture, the entr'acte and as a 'play-out' while the audience was leaving the theatre. The other numbers in the show, several of which were charming, were to fend for themselves and only three of them were ever published. In earlier days the complete vocal score of a musical comedy was published as a matter of course, in addition to which a booklet of the lyrics could be bought in the theatre with the programme. These little paper-bound books were well worth the sixpence charged because they helped those with a musical ear to recapture more easily the tunes they wanted to remember and to set them in their minds.

In the years immediately preceding the first world war the American Invasion began innocuously with a few isolated song hits until Irving Berlin established a beach-head with 'Alexander's Ragtime Band'. English composers, taken by surprise and startled by vital Negro-Jewish rhythms from the New World, fell back in some disorder; conservative musical opinion was shocked and horrified by such alien noises and, instead of saluting the new order and welcoming the new vitality, turned up its patrician nose and retired disgruntled from the arena.

At this moment war began, and there was no longer any time. It is reasonable to suppose that a large number of potential young composers were wiped out in those sad years and that had they not been, the annihilation of English light music would not have been so complete. As it was, when finally the surviving boys came home, it was to an occupied country; the American victory was a *fait accompli*. This obviously was the moment for British talent to rally, to profit by defeat, to absorb and utilize the new, exciting rhythms from over the water and to modify and adapt them to its own service, but apparently this was either beyond our capacity or we were too tired to attempt it. At all events, from the nineteen-twenties until today, there have been few English composers of light music capable of creating an integrated score.

One outstanding exception was the late Ivor Novello. His primary talent throughout his whole life was music, and 'Glamorous Night', 'Arc de Triomphe', 'The Dancing Years', 'Perchance to Dream' and 'King's Rhapsody' were rich in melody and technically expert. For years he upheld, almost alone, our old traditions of musical Musical Comedy. His principal tunes were designed, quite deliberately, to catch the ear of the public and, being simple, sentimental, occasionally conventional but always melodic, they invariably achieved their object. The rest of his scores, the openings, finales, choral interludes and incidental themes he wrote to please himself and in these, I believe, lay his true quality; a much finer quality than most people realized. The fact that his music never received the critical acclaim that it deserved was irritating but unimportant. One does not expect present-day dramatic critics to know much about music; as a matter of fact one no longer expects them to know much about drama. Vivian Ellis has also proved over the years that he can handle a complete score with grace and finesse. 'Bless the Bride' was much more than a few attractive songs strung together and so, from the

musical standpoint, was 'Tough at the Top', although the show on the whole was a commercial failure.

Harold Fraser-Simson, who composed 'The Maid of the Mountains' and Frederic Norton, who composed 'Chu Chin Chow', are remembered only for these two outstanding scores. Their other music, later or earlier, is forgotten except by a minority.

I now arrive at the moment when willy-nilly I must discuss, as objectively as possible, my own contributions to this particular field. I have, within the last twenty-five years, composed many successful songs and three integrated scores of which I am genuinely proud. These are 'Bitter Sweet', 'Conversation Piece', and 'Pacific 1860'. 'This Year of Grace' and 'Words and Music', although revues, were also well constructed musically. 'Operette' was sadly meagre with the exception of three numbers, 'Dearest Love', 'Where are the Songs we Sung?' and 'The Stately Homes of England'. This latter, however, being a comedy quartette, relied for its success more on its lyrics than its tune. 'Ace of Clubs' contained several good songs, but could not fairly be described as a musical score. 'Sigh No More', 'On with the Dance' and 'London Calling' are outside this discussion as they were revues containing contributions from other composers. 'Bitter Sweet', the most flamboyantly successful of all my musical shows, had a full and varied score greatly enhanced by the orchestrations of Orrelana. 'Conversation Piece' was less full and varied but had considerable quality. With these two scores Miss Elsie April, to whom I dictated them, was a tremendous help to me both in transcribing and in sound musical advice. 'Pacific 1860' was, musically my best work to date. It was carefully balanced and well constructed and imaginatively orchestrated by Ronald Binge and Mantovani. The show, as a whole, was a failure. It had been planned on a small scale, but, owing to theatre exigencies and other circumstances, had to be blown up to fit the stage of Drury Lane. The Press blasted the book, hardly mentioned the music or lyrics, and that was that. It closed after a few months.

Proceeding on the assumption that the reader of this preface is interested in the development of my musical talent, I will try to explain, as concisely as I can, how, in this respect, my personal wheels go round. To begin with, I have only had two music lessons in my life. These were the first steps of what was to have been a full course at the Guildhall School of Music, and they faltered and stopped when I was told by my instructor that I could not use consecutive fifths. He went on to explain that a gentleman called Ebenezer Prout had announced many years ago that consecutive fifths were wrong and must in no circumstances be employed. At that time Ebenezer Prout was merely a name to me (as a matter of fact he still is, and a very funny one at that) and I was unimpressed by his Victorian dicta. I argued back that Debussy and Ravel used consecutive fifths like mad. My instructor waved aside this triviality with a pudgy hand, and I left his presence for ever with the parting shot that what was good enough for Debussy and Ravel was good enough for me. This outburst of rugged individualism deprived me of much valuable knowledge, and I have never deeply regretted it for a moment. Had I intended at the outset of my career to devote all my energies to music I would have endured the necessary training cheerfully enough, but in those days I was passionately involved in the theatre; acting and writing and singing and dancing seemed of more value to my immediate progress than counterpoint and harmony. I was willing to allow the musical side of my creative talent to take care of itself. On looking back, I think that on the whole I was right. I have often been irritated in later years by my inability to write music down effectively and by my complete lack of knowledge of orchestration except by ear, but being talented from the very beginning in several different media, I was forced by common sense to make a decision. The decision I made was to try to become a good writer and actor, and to compose tunes and harmonies whenever the urge to do so became too powerful to resist.

I have never been unduly depressed by the fact that all my music has to be dictated. Many famous light composers never put so much as a crotchet* on paper. To be born with a natural ear for music is a great and glorious gift. It is no occasion for pride and it has nothing to do with will-power, concentration or industry. It is either there or it isn't. What is so curious is that it cannot, in any circumstances, be wrong where one's own harmonies are concerned. In New York, when I was recording 'Conversation Piece' with Lily Pons, I detected a false note in the orchestration. It happened to be in a very fully scored passage and the mistake was consequently difficult to trace. The orchestrator, the conductor and the musical producer insisted that I was wrong; only Lily Pons, who has perfect pitch, backed me up. Finally, after much argument and fiddle-faddle it was discovered that the oboe was playing an A flat instead of an A natural. The greatness and gloriousness of this gift, however, can frequently be offset by excruciating discomfort. On many occasions in my life I have had to sit smiling graciously while some well-meaning but inadequate orchestra obliges with a selection from my works. Cascades of wrong notes lacerate my nerves, a flat wind instrument pierces my ear-drums, and though I continue to smile appreciatively, the smile, after a little while, becomes tortured and looks as if my mouth were filled with lemon juice.

I could not help composing tunes even if I wished to. Ever since I was a little boy they have dropped into my mind unbidden and often in the most unlikely circumstances. The 'Bitter Sweet' waltz, 'I'll See You Again', came to me whole and complete in a taxi when I was appearing in New York in 'This Year of Grace'. I was on my way home to my apartment after a matinée and had planned, as usual, to have an hour's rest and a light dinner before the evening performance. My taxi got stuck in a traffic block on the corner of Broadway and Seventh Avenue, klaxons were honking, cops were shouting and suddenly in the general din there was the melody, clear and unmistakable. By the time I got home the words of the first phrase had emerged. I played it over and over again on the piano (key of E flat as usual) and tried to rest, but I was too excited to sleep.

Oddly enough, one of the few songs I ever wrote that came to me in a setting appropriate to its content was 'Mad Dogs and Englishmen'. This was conceived and executed during a two-thousand-mile car drive from Hanoi in Tonkin to the Siamese border.

The birth of 'I'll Follow my Secret Heart' was even more surprising. I was working on 'Conversation Piece' at Goldenhurst, my home in Kent. I had completed some odd musical phrases here and there but no main waltz theme, and I was firmly and miserably stuck. I had sat at the piano daily for hours, repeatedly trying to hammer out an original tune or even an arresting first phrase, and nothing had resulted from my concentrated efforts but banality. I knew that I could never complete the score without my main theme as a pivot and finally, after ten days' increasing despair, I decided to give up and, rather than go on flogging myself any further, postpone the whole project for at least six months. This would entail telegraphing to Yvonne Printemps who was in Paris waiting eagerly for news and telling Cochran who had already announced the forthcoming production in the Press. I felt fairly wretched but at least relieved that I had had the sense to admit failure while there was still time. I poured myself a large whisky and soda, dined in grey solitude, poured myself another, even larger, whisky and soda, and sat gloomily envisaging everybody's disappointment and facing the fact that my talent had withered and that I should never write any more music until the day I died. The whisky did little to banish my gloom, but there was no more work to be done and I didn't care if I became fried as a coot, so I gave myself another drink and decided to go to bed. I switched off the lights at the door and noticed that there was one lamp left on by the piano. I walked automatically to turn it off, sat down and played 'I'll Follow my Secret Heart', straight through in E flat, a key I had never played in before.

*quarter-note

There is, to me, strange magic in such occurrences. I am willing and delighted to accept praise for my application, for my self-discipline and for my grim determination to finish a thing once I have started it. My acquired knowledge is praiseworthy, too, for I have worked hard all my life to perfect the material at my disposal. But these qualities, admirable as they undoubtedly are, are merely accessories. The essential talent is what matters and essential talent is unexplainable. My mother and father were both musical in a light, amateur sense, but their gift was in no way remarkable. My father, although he could improvise agreeably at the piano, never composed a set piece of music in his life. I have known many people who were tone-deaf whose parents were far more actively musical than mine. I had no piano lessons when I was a little boy except occasionally from my mother who tried once or twice, with singular lack of success, to teach me my notes. I could, however, from the age of about seven onwards, play any tune I had heard on the piano in the pitch dark. To this day my piano-playing is limited to three keys: E flat, B flat and A flat. The sight of two sharps frightens me to death.

When I am in the process of composing anything in the least complicated I can play it in any key on the keyboard, but I can seldom if ever repeat these changes afterwards unless I practise them assiduously every day. In E flat I can give the impression of playing well. A flat and B flat I can get away with, but if I have to play anything for the first time it is always to my beloved E flat that my fingers move automatically. Oddly enough, C major, the key most favoured by the inept, leaves me cold. It is supposed to be easier to play in than any of the others because it has no black notes, but I have always found it dull. Another of my serious piano-playing defects is my left hand.

Dear George Gershwin used to moan at me in genuine distress and try to force my fingers on to the right notes. As a matter of fact he showed me a few tricks that I can still do, but they are few and dreadfully far between. I can firmly but not boastfully claim that I am a better pianist than Irving Berlin, but as that superlative genius of light music is well known not to be able to play at all except in C major, I will not press the point. Jerome D. Kern, to my mind one of the most inspired romantic composers of all, played woodenly as a rule and without much mobility. Dick Rodgers plays his own music best when he is accompanying himself or someone else, but he is far from outstanding. Vincent Youmans was a marvellous pianist, almost as brilliant as Gershwin, but these are the only two I can think of who, apart from their creative talent, could really play.

At the very beginning of this introduction I said that I was born into a generation that took light music seriously. It was fortunate for me that I was, because by the time I had emerged from my teens the taste of the era had changed. In my early twenties and thirties it was from America that I gained my greatest impetus. In New York they have always taken light music seriously. There, it is, as it should be, saluted as a specialized form of creative art, and is secure in its own right. The basis of a successful American musical show is now and has been for many years its music and its lyrics. Here in England there are few to write the music and fewer still to recognize it when it is written. The commercial managers have to fill their vast theatres and prefer, naturally enough, to gamble on acknowledged Broadway successes rather than questionable home products. The critics are quite incapable of distinguishing between good light music and bad light music, and the public are so saturated with the cheaper outpourings of Tin Pan Alley, which are dinned into their ears interminably by the B.B.C., that their natural taste will soon die a horribly unnatural death. It is a depressing thought, but perhaps some day soon, someone, somewhere, will appear with an English musical so strong in native quality that it will succeed in spite of the odds stacked against it.

Sir Noël Coward, in a recent interview, was asked his idea of a perfect life. Without hesitation he replied, "Mine." And a *perfect* tribute to Sir Noël has been realized in OH, COWARD!, the delightful off-Broadway revue which opened at the New Theatre, October 4, 1972. The show, devised and directed by Roderick Cook (who also appears in it), runs the gamut of Coward's way with words and music, capturing in but two short hours the true essence and magic of Noël Coward.

WRODERICK PRODUCTIONS PRESENT

BARBARA CASON   **RODERICK COOK**   **JAMIE ROSS**

In

A NEW MUSICAL COMEDY REVUE

Words and Music by **NOËL COWARD**

Settings by **HELEN POND** and **HERBERT SENN**
Musical Direction and Arrangements by **RENE WIEGERT**

Production Stage Manager by Jay Leo Colt
Additional Musical Arrangements by Herbert Helbig and Nicholas Deutsch

Devised and Directed by **RODERICK COOK**

CONTENTS

Dance, Little Lady

"THIS YEAR OF GRACE"

NOËL COWARD

Allegretto

Moderato e tranquillo

Though you're on-ly sev-en-teen Far too much of life you've seen,

Syn-co-pa - ted child.

May-be if you on-ly knew where your path is lead-ing to

You'd be-come less wild; But I know it's vain try-ing to ex-plain,

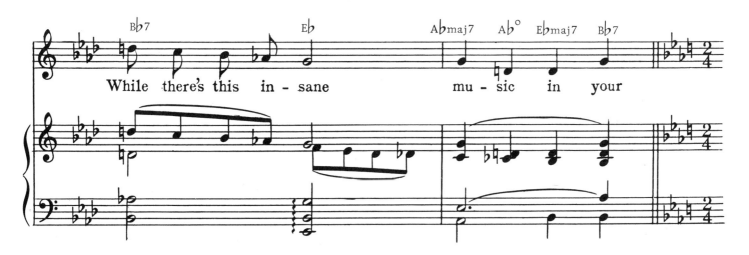

While there's this in-sane mu-sic in your

Tempo I

brain.

REFRAIN
Allegretto grazioso

Dance, dance, dance, lit-tle la-dy! Youth is fleet - ing to the

rhy - thm beat - ing In your mind. _____

Dance, dance, dance, lit-tle la-dy, So ob-sessed __ with sec-ond

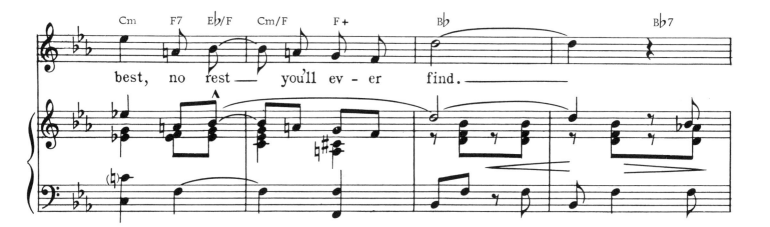

best, no rest ___ you'll ev - er find. ___

Time and tide and trou - ble nev - er, nev - er wait,

Let the caul-dron bub - ble, Just - i - fy your fate. Dance, dance,

dance, lit - tle la - dy! Dance, dance, dance, lit - tle la - dy! Leave to - mor-

_ row be - hind.

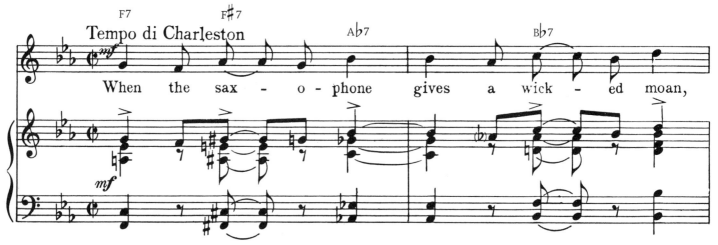

Tempo di Charleston

When the sax - o - phone gives a wick - ed moan,

Charles - ton _ Hey! Hey! _ Rhy - thms _ fall and _ rise,

Start danc - ing to the tune _ the band's

croon - ing —— for soon the night —— will be gone.

Start sway - ing like a reed— with-out heed - ing the speed that hur-

- ries you on. Nig - ger mel - o - dies

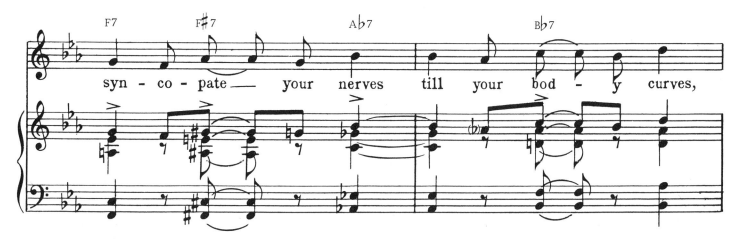

syn - co - pate—— your nerves till your bod - y curves,

Droop - ing, ___ stoop - ing, ___ Laugh - ter ___ some day ___

dies, _____ And when the lights are start - ing to

gut - ter Dawn through the shut - ter

shows you're liv - ing in a world of lies. ___

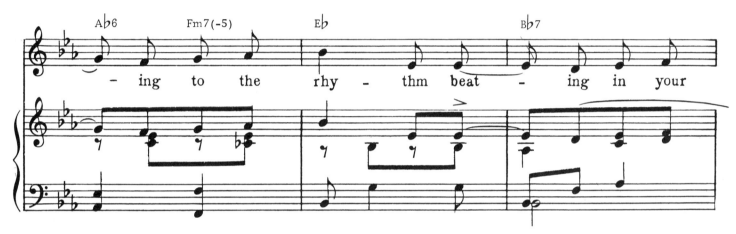

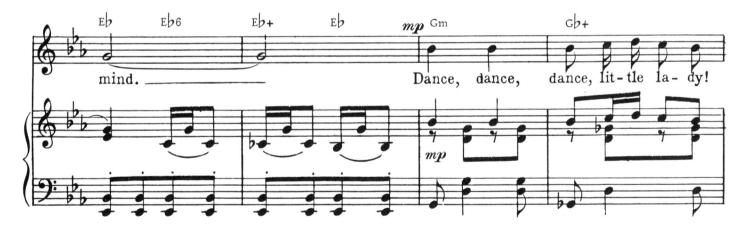

find. _____ Time and tide and trou-ble

nev - er, nev - er wait, Let the caul - dron

bub - ble, Just - i - fy your fate.

Dance, dance, dance, lit - tle la - dy! Dance, dance,

dance, lit - tle la - dy! Leave your troub - les be -

hind.

hind.

A Room With A View

"THIS YEAR OF GRACE"

NOËL COWARD

I've been cher-ish-ing Through the per-ish-ing win-ter nights and

days A fun-ny lit-tle phrase, That means ___

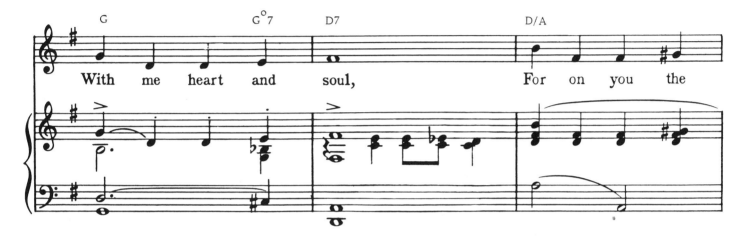

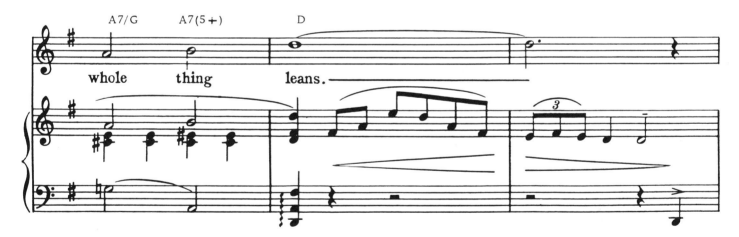

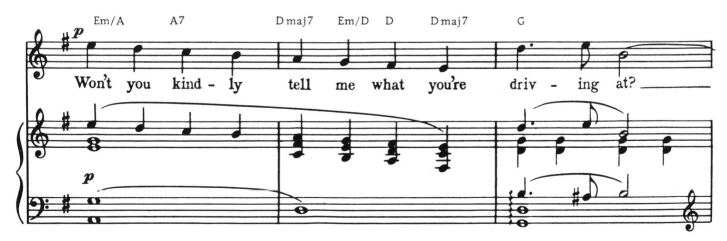

What con - clu - sion you're ar -

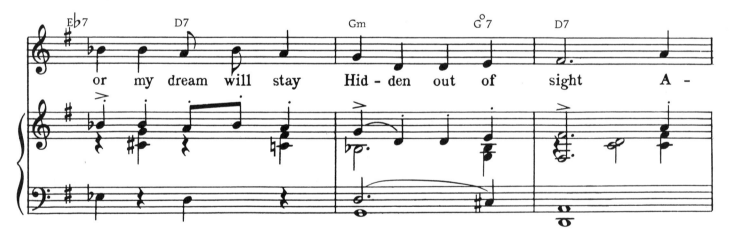

riv - ing at?_____ Please don't turn a - way

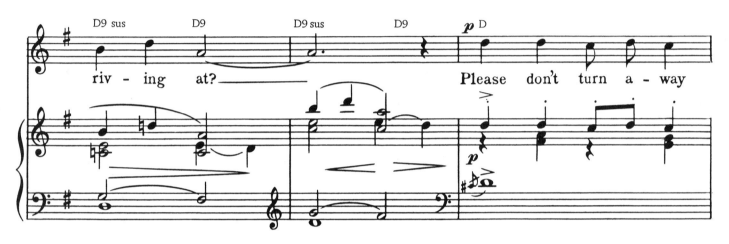

or my dream will stay Hid - den out of sight A -

mong a lot of might - have - beens!

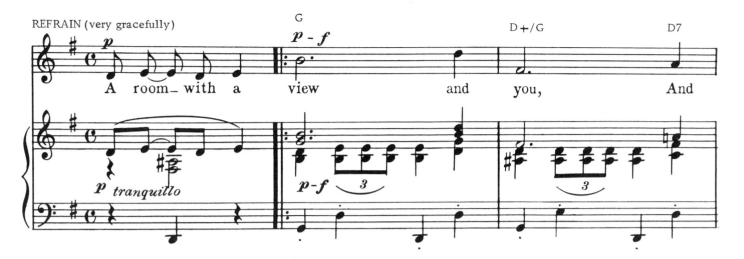

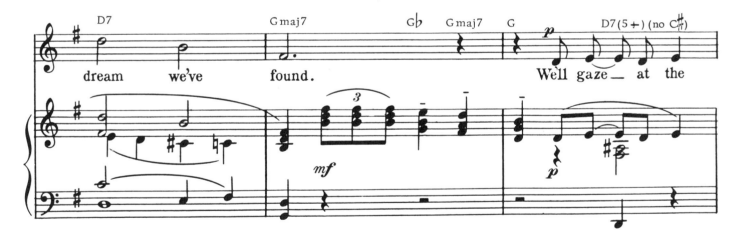

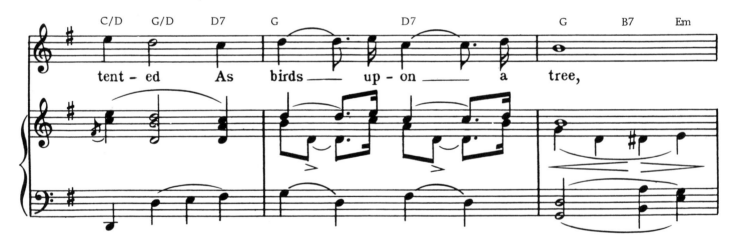

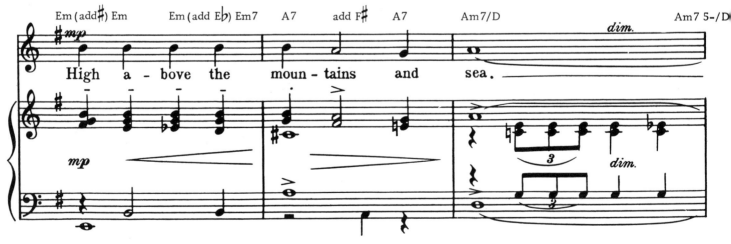

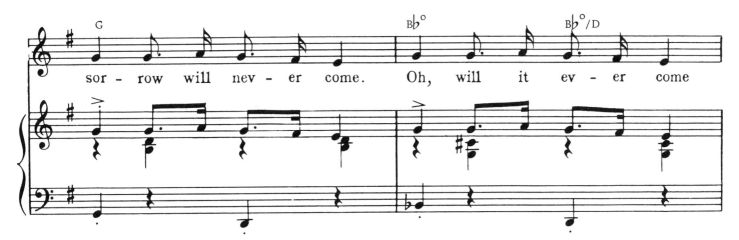

World Weary

"THIS YEAR OF GRACE"

NOËL COWARD

When I'm feel-ing drear-y and blue I'm on-ly too glad to be left a-lone,
Get up in the morn-ing at eight, Re-lent-less Fate Drives me to work at nine;

Dream-ing of a place in the sun when day— is done,
Toil-ing like a bee in a hive From four— to five,

Far from a tel-e-phone; Bus-tle and the wear-y crowd,
Wheth-er it's wet or fine, Hard-ly ev-er see the sky,

Make me want to cry out loud. Give me some-thing peace-ful and
Build-ings seem to grow so high. May - be in the fu - ture I

grand Where all — the land slum-bers in mo - no - tone. I'm
will Per - haps— ful - fill This lit - tle dream of mine. I'm

REFRAIN (not fast)

world wear-y, world wear-y, Liv - ing in a great big
world wear-y, world wear-y, Liv - ing in a great big

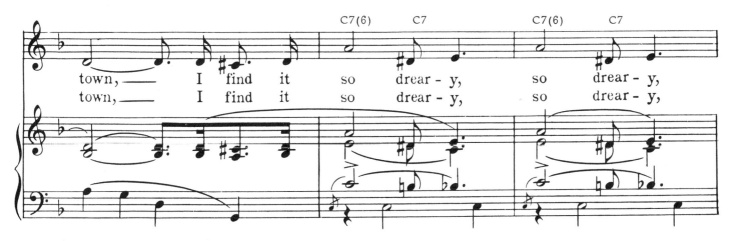

town, —— I find it so drear - y, so drear - y,
town, —— I find it so drear - y, so drear - y,

Ev - 'ry-thing looks grey or brown.___ I want an o - cean blue,
Ev - 'ry-thing looks grey or brown.___ I want a horse and plough,

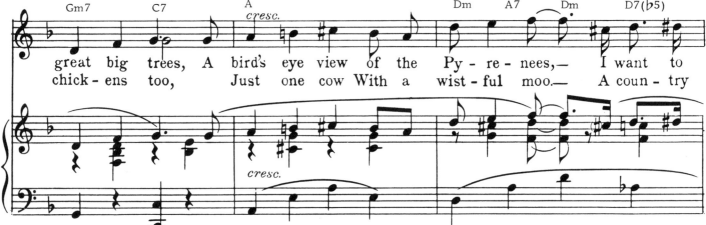

great big trees, A bird's eye view of the Py - re - nees,— I want to
chick - ens too, Just one cow With a wist-ful moo.— A coun - try

watch the moon rise up — And see the great red sun go down.
where the verb "to work"— Be-comes a most im-prop-er noun.

Watch - ing clouds go by through a wint - ry sky fas-cin - ates me,
I can hard-ly wait 'Till I see the great op-en spac - es,

But if I'm
My lov - ing

If Love Were All

"BITTER SWEET"

NOËL COWARD

29

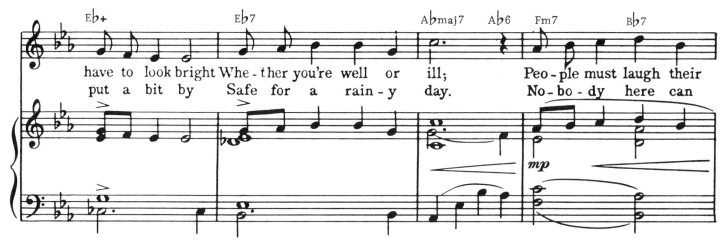

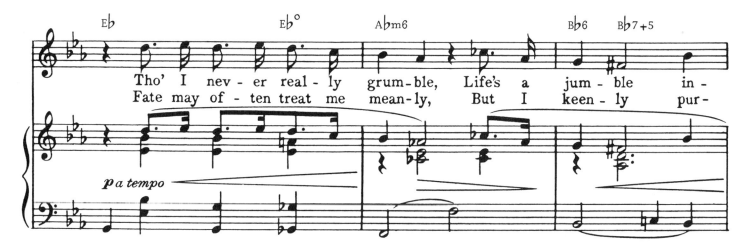

REFRAIN (plaintively)

lone - ly. I be - lieve the more you love a man. The

more you give your trust, The more you're bound to lose: Al - though ___

— when sha - dows fall _____ I think if on - ly

Some - bo - dy splen - did real - ly need - ed me, Some - one af - fec - tion - ate and

"Bitter Sweet" (1929) - PEGGY WOOD and GEORGE METAXA sing "I'll See You Again"

I'll See You Again

"BITTER SWEET"

Noël Coward

Moderato

To be-gin with, if you please, Sing a scale for me.

Take a breath and then re-prise in a dif-f'rent key. All my

life I shall re-mem - ber know-ing you; All the pleas-ure I have found in

show-ing you The dif-f'rent ways that one may phrase,

The chang-ing light and chang-ing shade, Hap-pi-ness that must die,

Mel-o-dies that must fly, Mem-o-ries that must fade, Dust-y and for-

got-ten by and by._____ Learn-ing scales will nev-er

seem so sweet a-gain Till our des-ti-ny shall let us meet_ a-gain.

Zigeuner

"BITTER SWEET"

Noël Coward

Once up-on a time, _____ Man-y years a-go _____
_ Lived a fair Prin-cess Hat-ing to con-fess Lone-li-ness was

tor - tur - ing her so.___ Then a gyp - sy came, Called to her by

name, Woo'd her with a song Sen - su - ous and strong. All the sum - mer

long Her pas - sion seemed to trem - ble like a liv - ing frame.

accel.

REFRAIN

Play to me be - neath the sum - mer moon, Zi - geu - -

allargando

a tempo

Someday I'll Find You

"PRIVATE LIVES"

NOËL COWARD

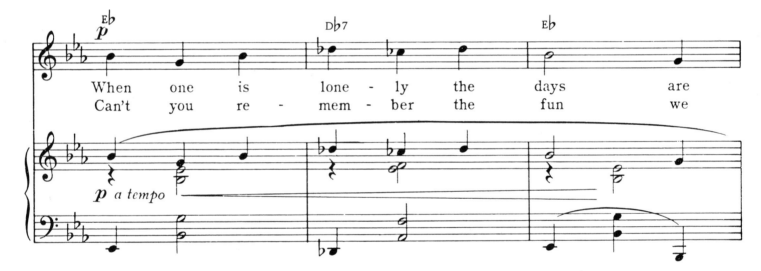

When one is lone - ly the days are
Can't you re - mem - ber the fun we

long; You seem so near,
had? Time is so fleet,

But nev - er ap - pear. Each night I
Why should - n't we meet? When you're a -

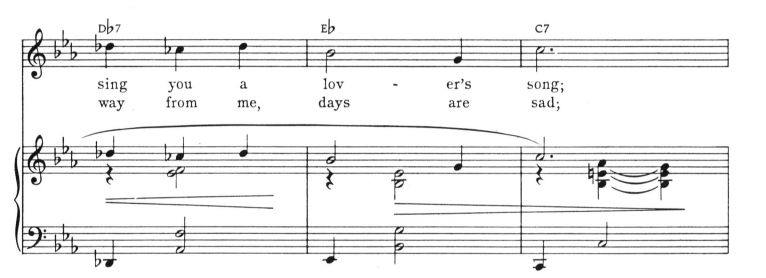

sing you a lov - er's song;
way from me, days are sad;

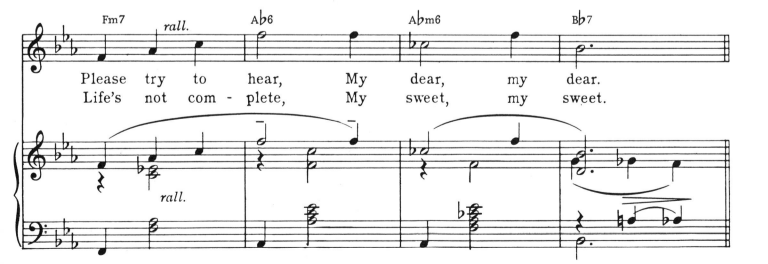

Please try to hear, My dear, my dear.
Life's not com - plete, My sweet, my sweet.

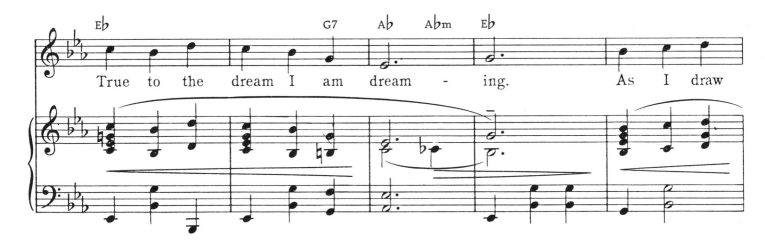

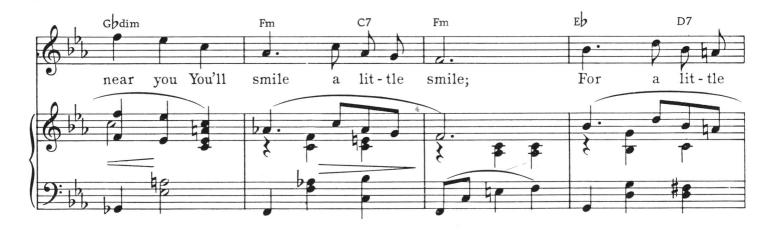

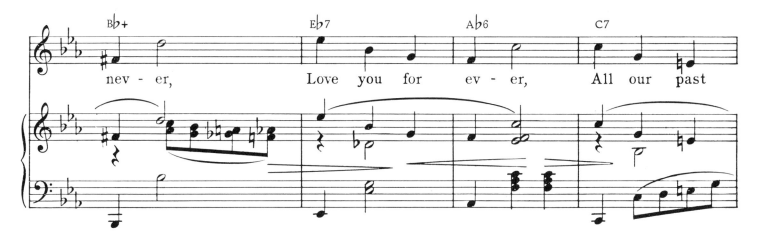

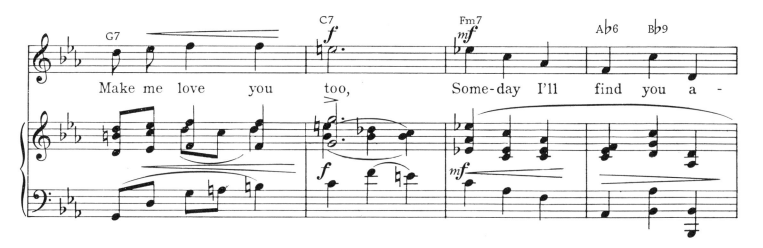

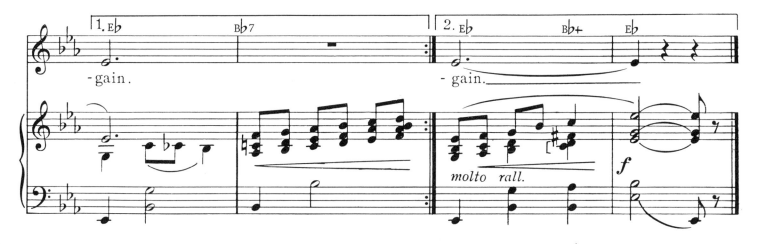

Let's Say Goodbye

NOËL COWARD

"WORDS AND MUSIC"

Now we've em - bark'd on this love af - fair, Don't let's des -

-troy it with tears, _____ Once we be - gin To let

REFRAIN

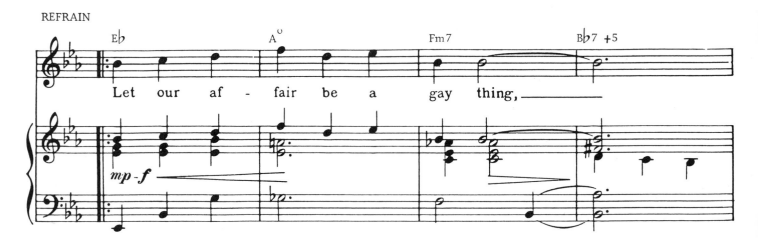

Let our af - fair be a gay thing,_____

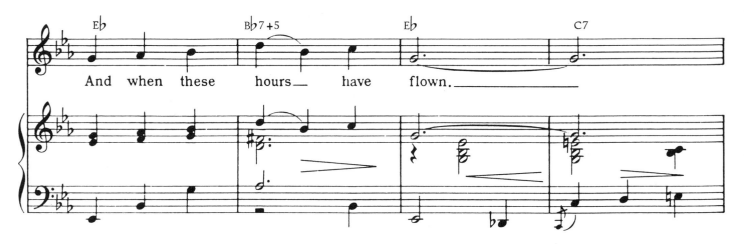

And when these hours__ have flown._____

Then, with-out for - get - ting Hap - pi - ness that has passed,

There'll be no re - gret - ting Fun that did - n't quite last.

Mad About The Boy

NOËL COWARD

"WORDS AND MUSIC"

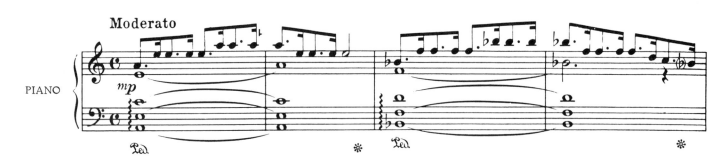

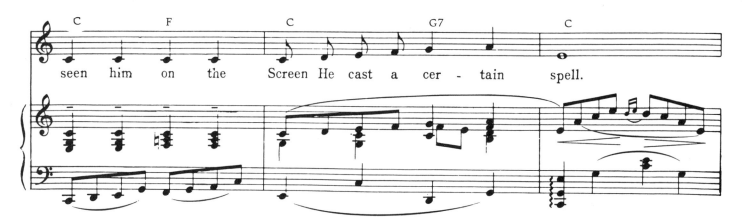

I bask'd in his at-trac-tion for a cou-ple of hours or so, His

man-ners were a frac-tion too met - i - cu - lous. If he was real or not I could - n't

tell, But like a sil - ly fool I fell.

REFRAIN

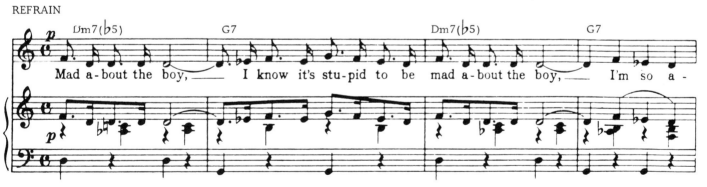

Mad a-bout the boy, ____ I know it's stu-pid to be mad a-bout the boy, ____ I'm so a-

shamed of it, But must ad-mit The sleep-less nights I've had a-bout the boy.

On the Sil-ver Screen He melts my fool-ish heart in ev-'ry sin-gle scene, Al-though I'm

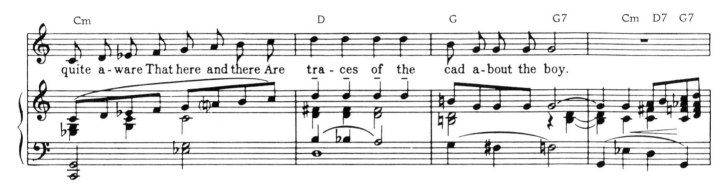

quite a-ware That here and there Are tra-ces of the cad a-bout the boy.

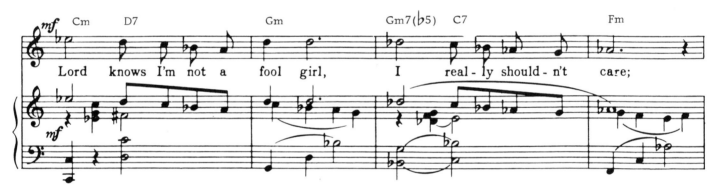

Lord knows I'm not a fool girl, I real-ly should-n't care;

Lord knows I'm not a school girl, In the flur-ry of her first af - fair.

Will it ev-er cloy?___ This odd di-ver-si-ty of mis-er-y and joy;___ I'm feel-ing

quite in-sane And young a-gain, And all be-cause I'm mad a-bout the boy.

It

seems a lit-tle sil-ly For a girl of my age and weight To walk down Pic-ca-dil-ly In a

haze of love, It ought to take a good deal more to get a bad girl down,

I should have been ex-empt, for My par-ti-cu-lar kind of Fate Has

taught me such con-tempt for Ev-'ry phase of love, And now I've been and spent my last half-

crown To weep a - bout a paint - ed clown.

Refrain

Mad a-bout the boy,____ It's pret-ty fun-ny, but I'm mad a-bout the boy.____ He has a

gay ap-peal That makes me feel There's may-be some-thing sad a-bout the boy.

Walk-ing down the street,____ His eyes look out at me from peo-ple that I meet;____ I can't be-

lieve it's true, But when I'm blue, In some strange way I'm glad a-bout the boy.

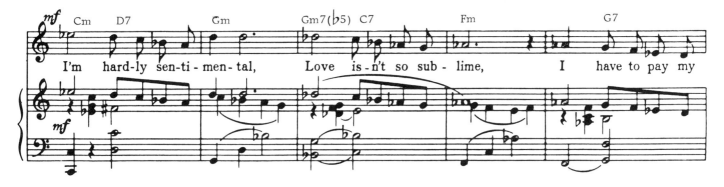

I'm hard-ly sen-ti-men-tal, Love is-n't so sub-lime, I have to pay my

rent-al And I can't af-ford to waste much time. If I could em-ploy___

___ A lit-tle ma-gic that would fin-al-ly de-stroy___ This dream that pains me And en-chains me, But I

can't, be-cause I'm mad a-bout the boy.

Mad Dogs And Englishmen

"WORDS AND MUSIC"

NOËL COWARD

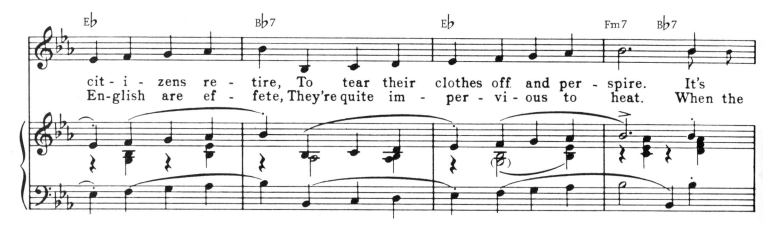

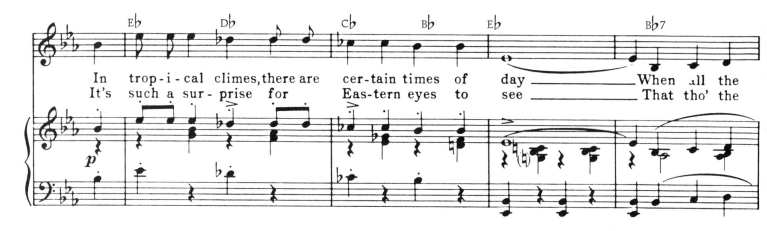

sun is much too sul - try, And one must a - void its ul - try - vi - 'let
sim - ple crea - tures hope he Will im - pale his Sol - ar To - pee on a

ray.
tree.

Pa - pa - la - ka, Pa - pa - la - ka, Pa - pa - la - ka boo! Pa - pa - la - ka, Pa - pa - la - ka, Pa - pa - la - ka boo!
Bo - ly - bo - ly, Bo - ly - bo - ly, Bo - ly - bo - ly baa! Bo - ly - bo - ly, Bo - ly - bo - ly, Bo - ly - bo - ly baa!

Di - ga - ri - ga, Di - ga - ri - ga, Di - ga - ri - ga doo! Di - ga - ri - ga, Di - ga - ri - ga,
Ha - ba - nin - ny, Ha - ba - nin - ny, Ha - ba - nin - ny haa! Ha - ba - nin - ny, Ha - ba - nin - ny,

Di - ga - ri - ga doo! The na - tives grieve, when the white men leave their huts;
Ha - ba - nin - ny haa! It seems such a shame when the En - glish claim the earth,

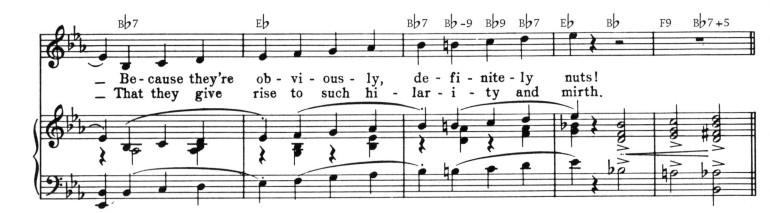

_ Be-cause they're ob - vi - ous - ly, de - fi - nite - ly nuts!
_ That they give rise to such hi - lar - i - ty and mirth.

REFRAIN

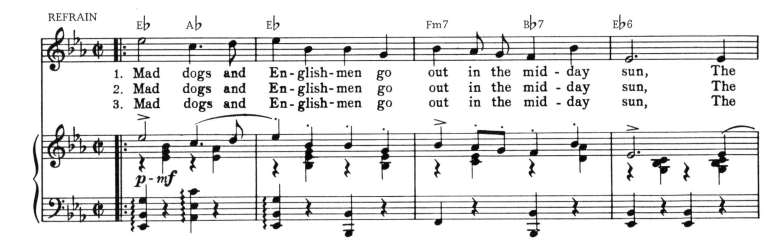

1. Mad dogs and En - glish-men go out in the mid - day sun, The
2. Mad dogs and En - glish-men go out in the mid - day sun, The
3. Mad dogs and En - glish-men go out in the mid - day sun, The

Jap - a - nese don't care to, The Chi - nese would-n't dare to. The Hin - dus and
tough-est Bur-mese ban-dit Can nev - er un - der stand it. In Ran - goon, the
small-est Ma - lay rab-bit De - plores this stu - pid hab - it. In Hong-kong, they

Ar - gen-tines sleep firm - ly from twelve to one, But En-glish-men de - test a si -
heat of noon Is just what the na - tives shun; They put their Scotch or Rye down and
strike a gong And fire off a noon-day gun, To rep-ri - mand each in-mate who's

The Party's Over Now

NOËL COWARD

"WORDS AND MUSIC"

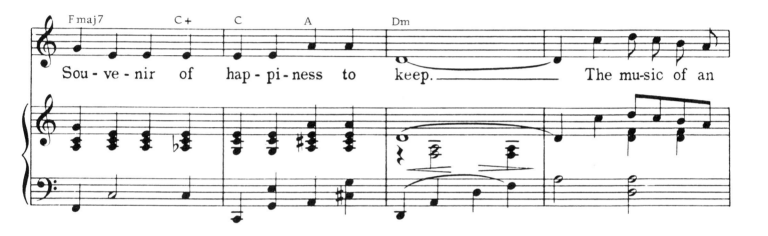

REFRAIN

Par - ty's o - ver now, The dawn is draw-ing ve-ry nigh,_____ The can-dles

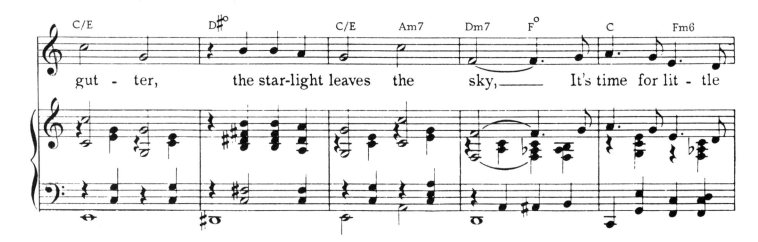

gut - ter, the star-light leaves the sky,_____ It's time for lit - tle

boys and girls To hur-ry home to bed,_____ For there's a new day

wait - ing just a - head._____ Life is sweet But

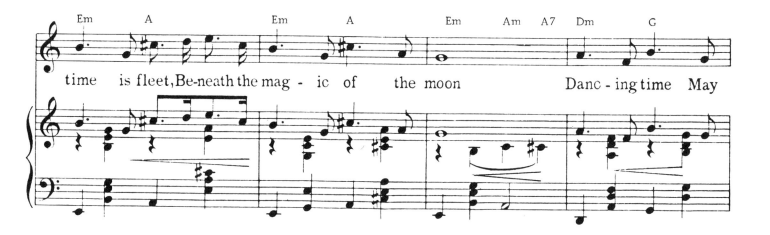

WORDS AND MUSIC (1932)

Top, Ivy St. Helier, Gerald Nodin, and Romney Brent

At left, Joyce Barbour and Chorus

CONVERSATION PIECE (1934)

Louis Hayward, Yvonne Printemps, Noël Coward, and Irene Browne

I'll Follow My Secret Heart

"CONVERSATION PIECE"

Noël Coward

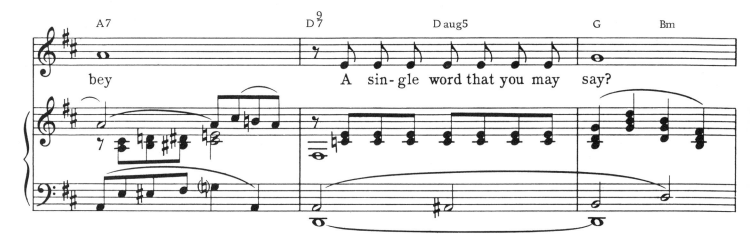

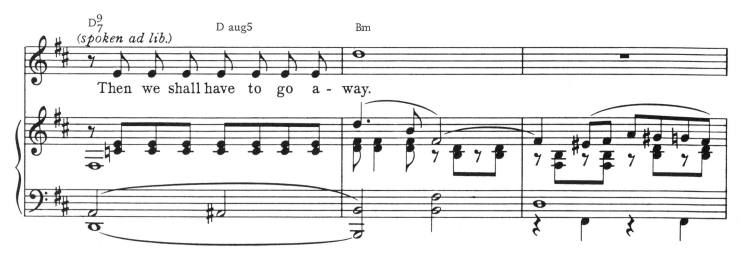

Don't be a-fraid I'll be-tray you And de-stroy all the plans you have

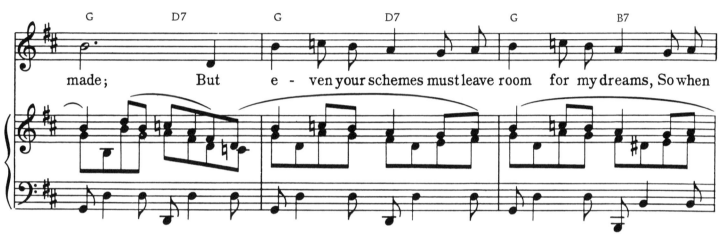

made; But e - ven your schemes must leave room for my dreams, So when

all I owe___ to you is paid, I'll still have some-thing of my

own, A lit-tle prize that's mine a - lone.

REFRAIN
(slow tempo di Valse)

I'll fol - low my se - cret heart my whole life

through,_____ I'll keep all my dreams a - part till

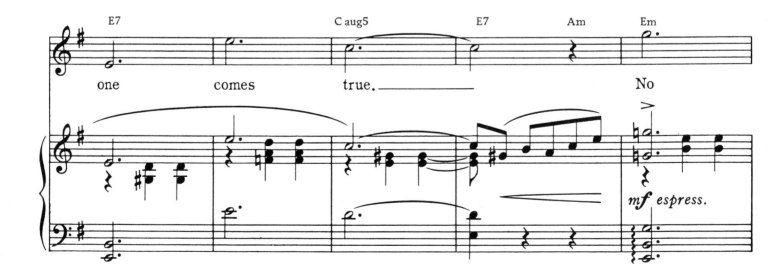

one comes true._____ No

mat - ter what price is paid, What stars may fade a - bove,____

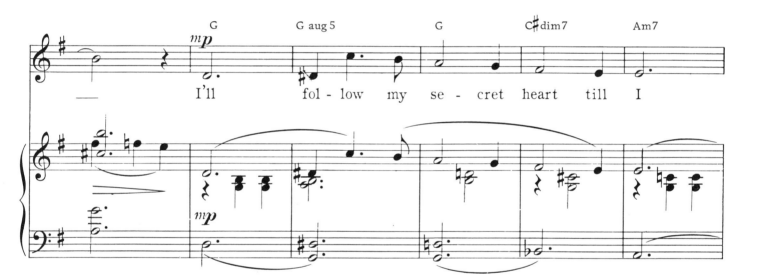

I'll fol - low my se - cret heart till I

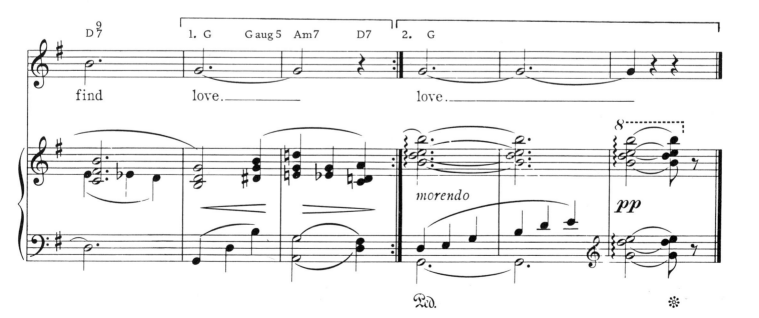

find love.____ love.____

Don't Put Your Daughter On The Stage,
Mrs. Worthington

NOËL COWARD

Don't put your daugh-ter on the stage, Mis-sis Worth-ing-ton;
Don't put your daugh-ter on the stage, Mis-sis Worth-ing-ton;

Don't put your daugh-ter on the stage._____ She's a
Don't put your daugh-ter on the stage._____ Tho' they

bit of an ug-ly duck-ling you must hon-est-ly con-fess, And the
said at the School of Act-ing she was love-ly as Peer Gynt I'm a-

width of her seat would sure-ly de-feat Her chan-ces of suc-cess. It's a
-fraid on the whole an in-gen-ue role Would em-pha-sise her squint. She's a

loud voice,___ and tho' it's not ex-act-ly flat She'll
big girl___ and tho' her teeth are fair-ly good She's

need a lit-tle more than that To earn a liv-ing wage. On my
not the type I ev-er would Be eag-er to en-gage. No more

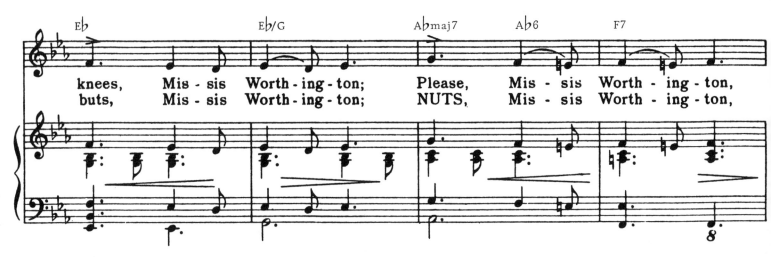

knees, Mis-sis Worth-ing-ton; Please, Mis-sis Worth-ing-ton,
buts, Mis-sis Worth-ing-ton; NUTS, Mis-sis Worth-ing-ton,

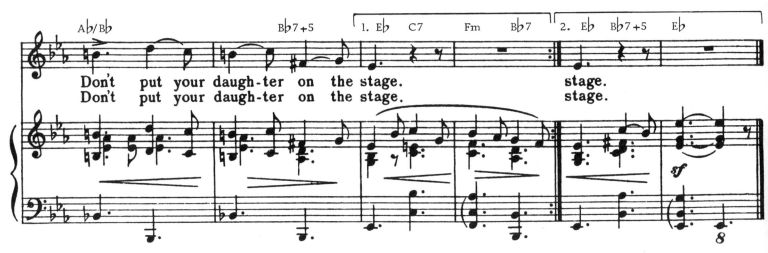

Don't put your daugh-ter on the stage. stage.
Don't put your daugh-ter on the stage. stage.

Play, Orchestra, Play

"TONIGHT AT 8:30"

NOËL COWARD

Lis-ten to the strain, it plays once more for us,

There it is a-gain — The past in store for us.

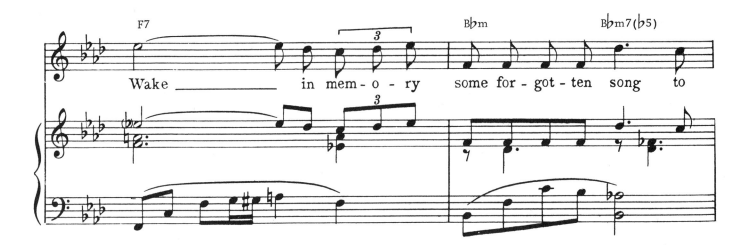

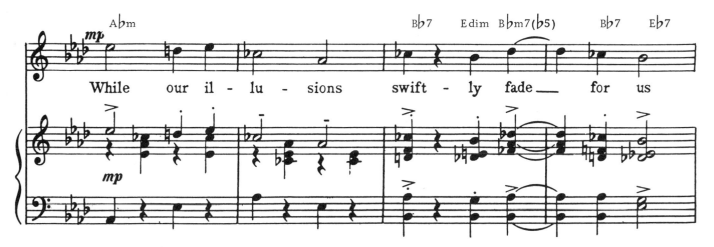

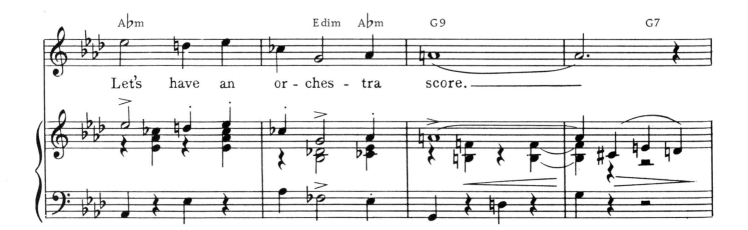

Let's have an or - ches - tra score.

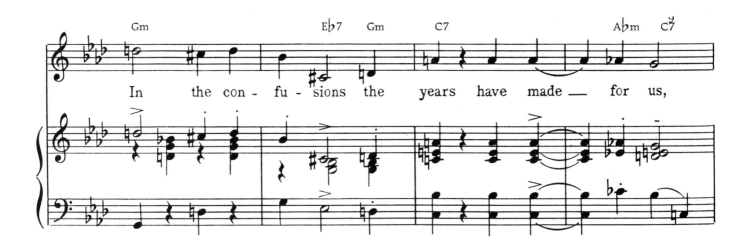

In the con - fu - sions the years have made — for us,

Ser - en - ade — for us just once more.

Life need - n't be grey,— al - though it's

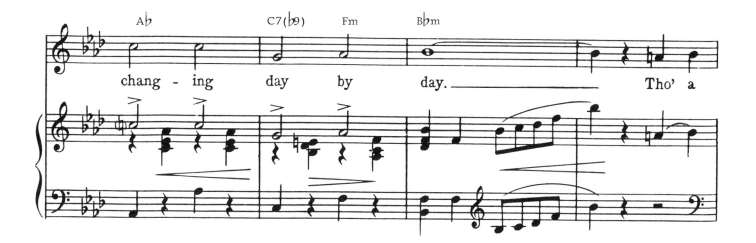

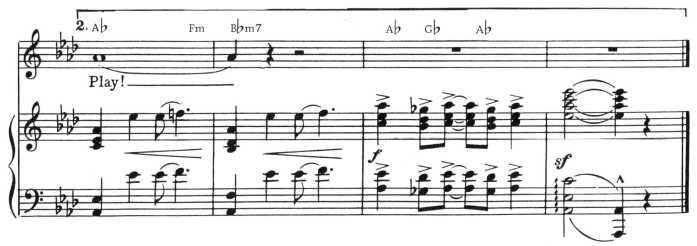

Has Anybody Seen Our Ship?

"TONIGHT AT 8:30"

NOËL COWARD

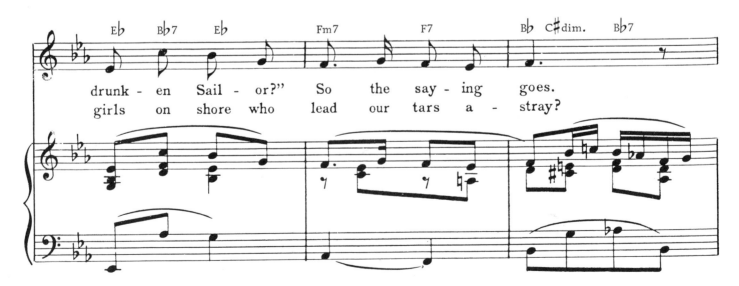

"What shall we do with the
What shall be done with the

drunk-en Sail-or?" So the say-ing goes.
girls on shore who lead our tars a-stray?

We're not tight but we're none too bright, Great Scott! I don't sup -
What's to be done with the drinks ga - lore That make them pass a -

pose. We've lost our way and we've lost our pay and to
way? We got wet ears from our first five beers, af - ter

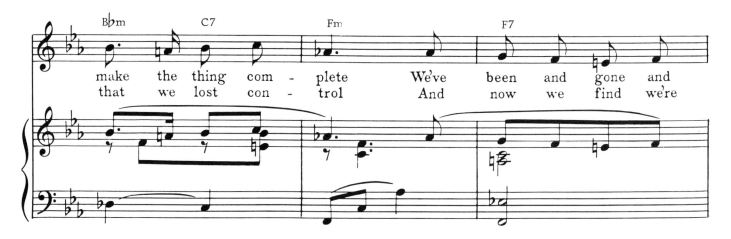

make the thing com - plete We've been and gone and
that we lost con - trol And now we find we're

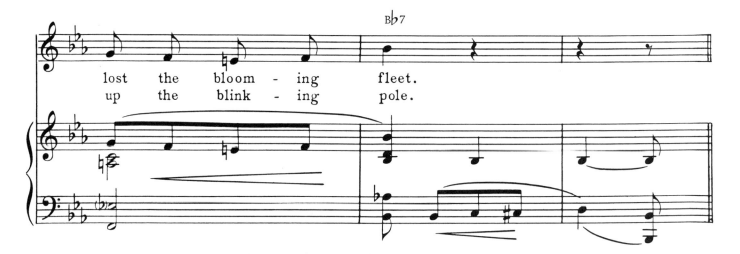

lost the bloom - ing fleet.
up the blink - ing pole.

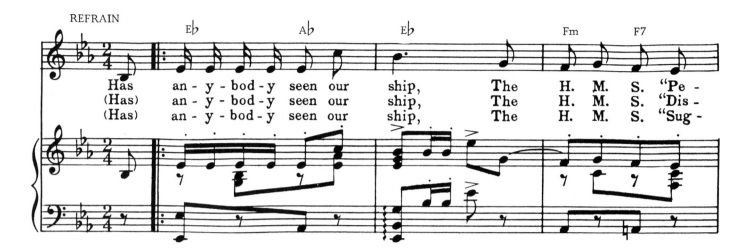

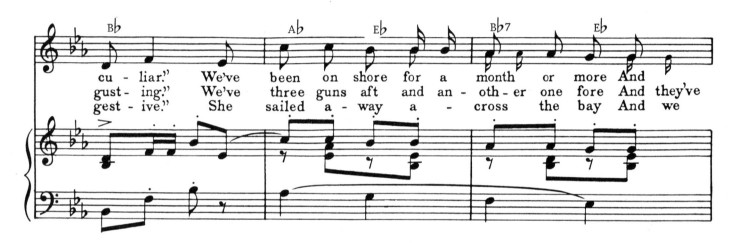

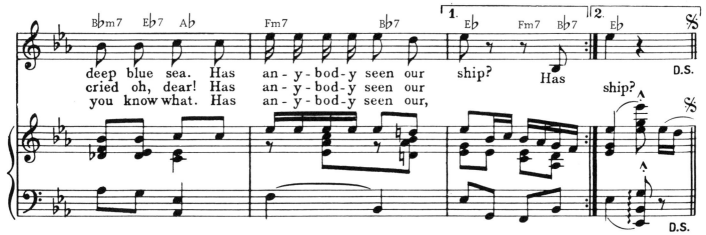

last time

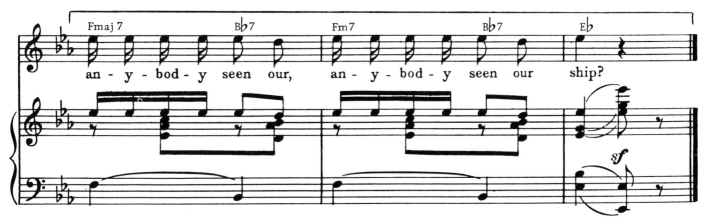

Men About Town

"TONIGHT AT 8:30"

NOËL COWARD

Nice and breezy

We're two chaps who find it thrill-ing to do the kill-ing, we're

al-ways will-ing to give the girls a treat_____ Just a drink at the Ritz,

call it double or quits, Then we feel the world is at our feet.

Top hats, white spats, Look di-vine on us, There's a shine on us, Get a line on us

when we come your way. Gad, e-lev-en o'-clock.

Let's pop in-to the "Troc" Ere we start the business of the day. As we

REFRAIN

stroll   down   Picc - Picc - a - dil - ly in   the
stroll   down   Picc - Picc - a - dil - ly all   the

bright morn - ing air _____ All the girls turn ____
girls say ____ "Who's here? _____ Put your hat straight!

____ and stare _____ We're so non - - cha -
____ my dear, _____ For it's Mar - - ma -

-lant ____ and fright-fully de - bon - air, When we chat
-duke ____ and Per - cy Vere - de - Vere". As we doff

to   Rose, Maud or Li - ly you should see the way their
hats   Each pret - ty Fil - ly gives a wink at us and

boy friends frown _____ For they know with-out a
then looks down _____ For they long with all their

doubt That their luck's right out Up a - gainst a cou - ple of
might For a red hot night When they see a cou - ple of

men a - bout Town.   As we Town. _____
men a - bout

We Were Dancing

"TONIGHT AT 8:30"

NOËL COWARD

feel con - ven - tion - al a - pol - o - gies are all in vain. You must see __

__ We've stepped in - to a dream That's set us free.

Don't think we planned it, Please un - der - stand it.

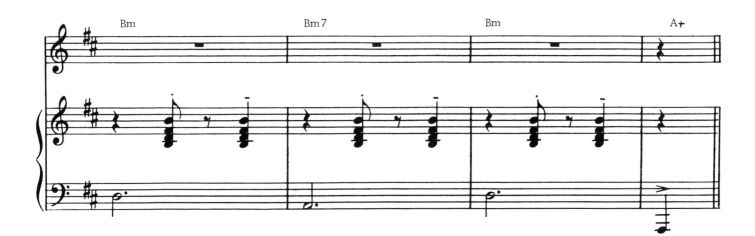

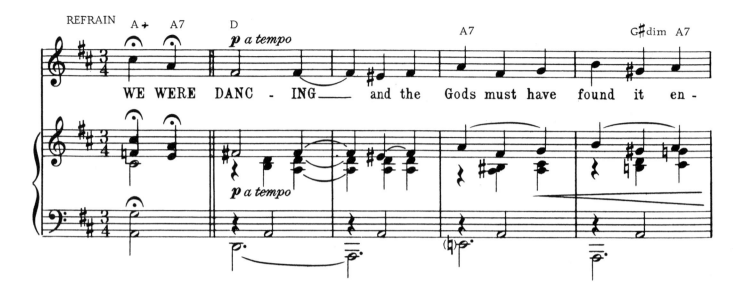

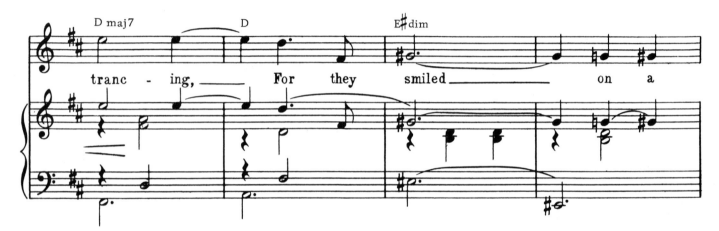

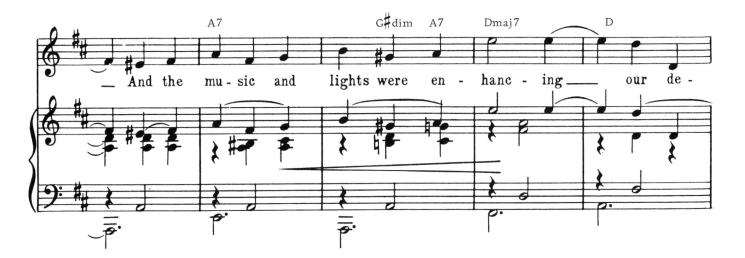

And the mu-sic and lights were en-hanc-ing____ our de-

sire _____ When the world _____ caught on fire _____

____ She and I were danc-ing.

Love lay in wait for us, Twist-ed our fate for us, No one

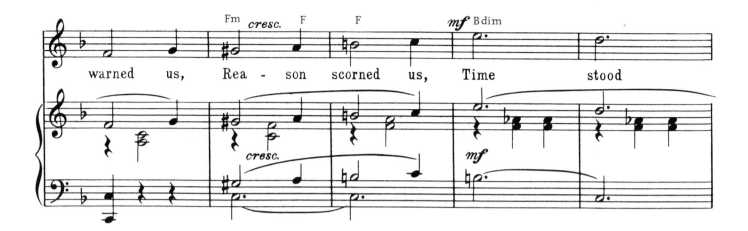

warned us, Rea - son scorned us, Time stood

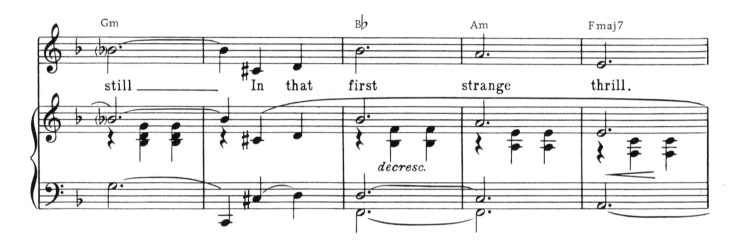

still _____ In that first strange thrill.

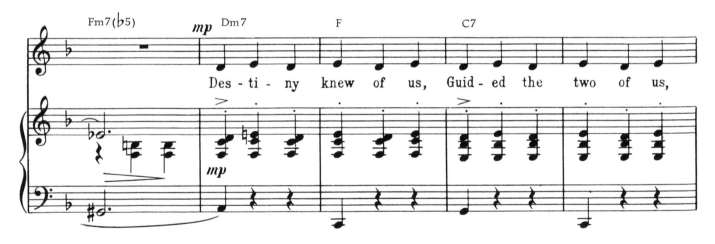

Des - ti - ny knew of us, Guid - ed the two of us,

How could we re - fuse to see that wrong

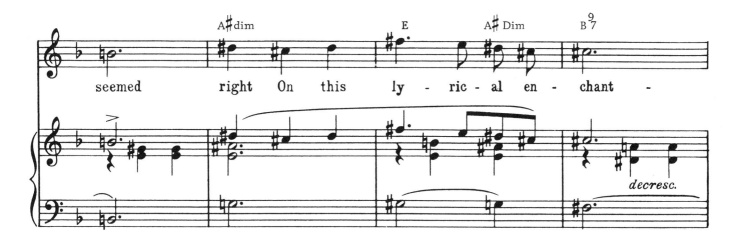

seemed right On this ly - ric - al en - chant -

ed night. _____ Log-ic sup - plies no

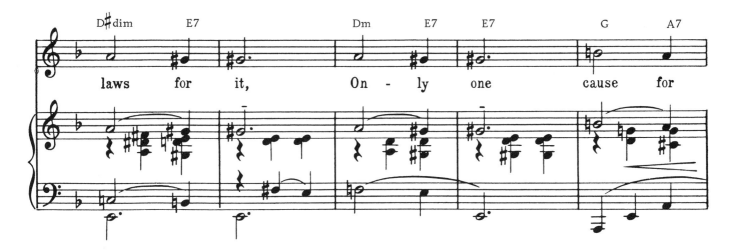

laws for it, On - ly one cause for

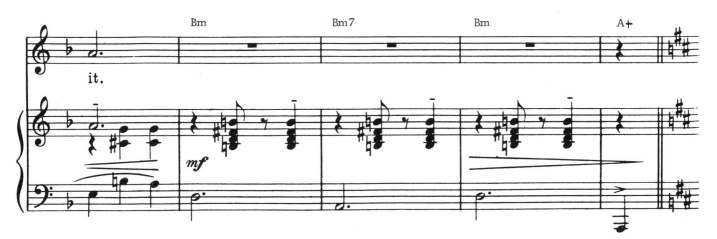

it.

Refrain

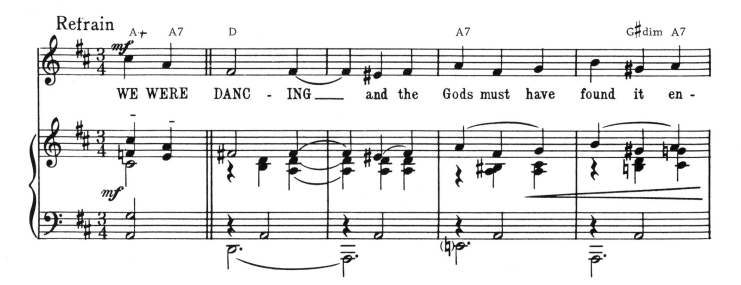

WE WERE DANC - ING__ and the Gods must have found it en -

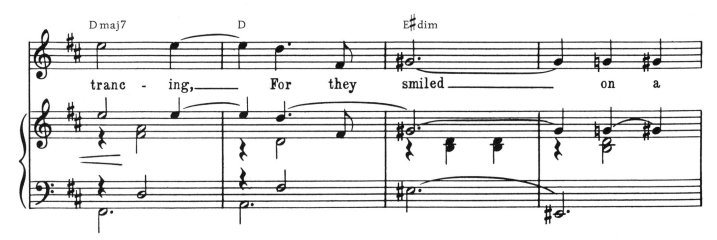

tranc - ing,__ For they smiled__ on a

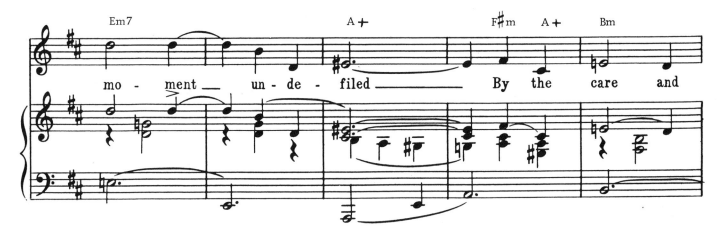

mo - ment __ un-de - filed __ By the care and

woe that mor - tals know, WE WERE DANC - ING__

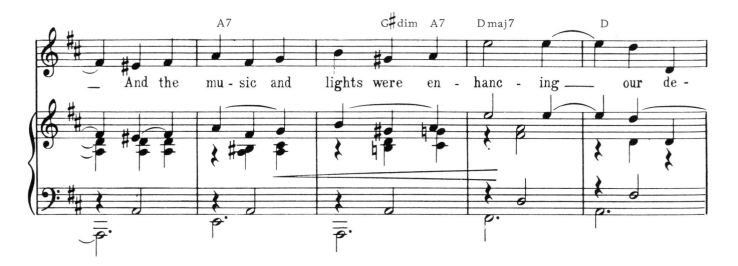

And the mu-sic and lights were en-hanc-ing____ our de-

sire_____ When the world_____ caught on fire_____

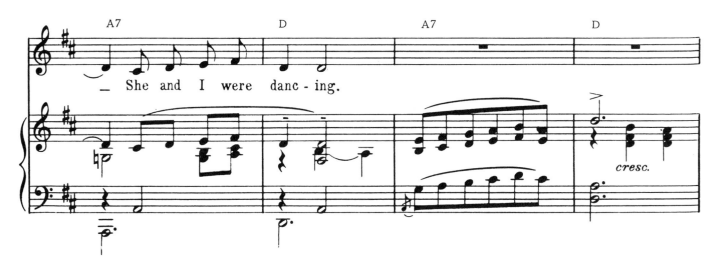

____ She and I were danc-ing.

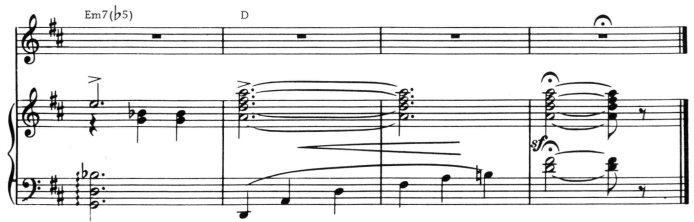

YOU WERE THERE

"TONIGHT AT 8:30"

NOËL COWARD

Was ___ it in the real world? Or was ___ it in a dream?
How ___ could we ex - plain it, The spark ___ and then the fire?

Was ___ it just a note ___ in some e - ter - nal theme?
How ___ add up the to - tal of our heart's de - sire?

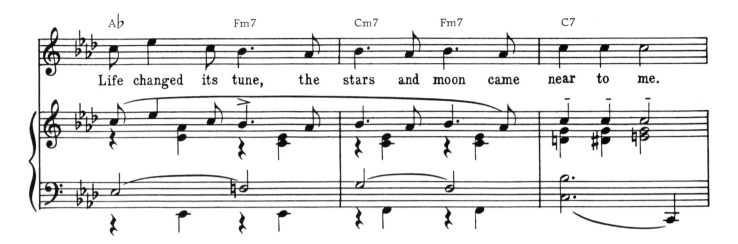

Life changed its tune, the stars and moon came near to me.

Dreams that I dreamed like mag - ic seemed to be

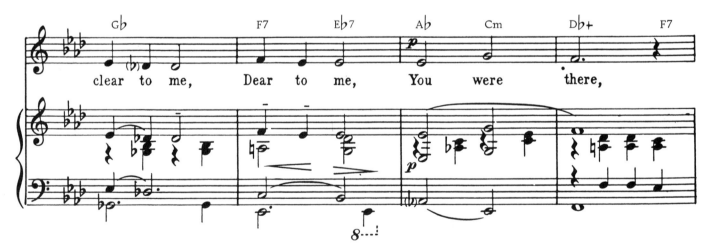

clear to me, Dear to me, You were there,

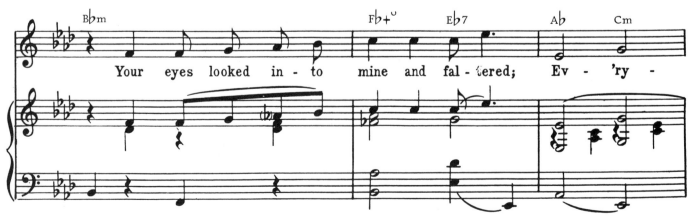

Your eyes looked in - to mine and fal - tered; Ev - 'ry -

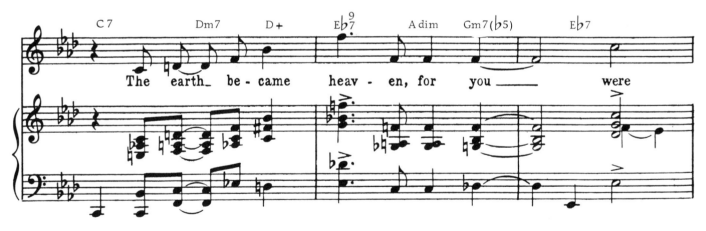

The Stately Homes Of England

Noël Coward

"OPERETTE"

Moderato

PIANO

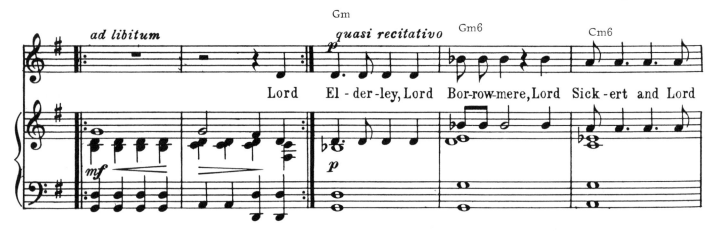

Lord El-der-ley, Lord Bor-row-mere, Lord Sick-ert and Lord

Camp With ev-'ry vir-tue, ev-'ry grace, Ah! what a-vails the scep-tred race.

Here you see___ the four of us, And there are so ma-ny more of us,
Here you see___ the pick of us, You may be heart-i-ly sick of us

Eld - est sons____ that must suc - ceed._____ We know how Cae - sar con - quer'd
Still with sense____ We're all im - bued,_____ We waste no time on vain re -

Gaul And how to whack a crick - et ball, A - part from this, our ed - u - ca - tion
grets And when we're forced to pay our debts We're al - ways a - ble to dis - pose of

Lacks co - or - di - na - tion. Tho' we're young____ and ten - ta - tive And rath - er
Rows and rows and rows of Gains - bor - oughs____ and Law - renc - es, Some sport - ing

rip - re - pre - sent - a - tive, Sci - ons of____ a no - ble breed,_____ We are the
prints of Aunt Flor - en - ce's, Some of which_ were rath - er rude._____ Al - tho' we

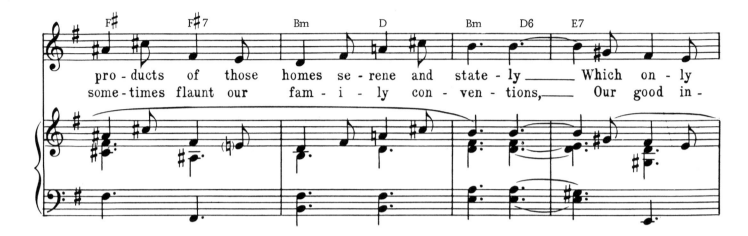

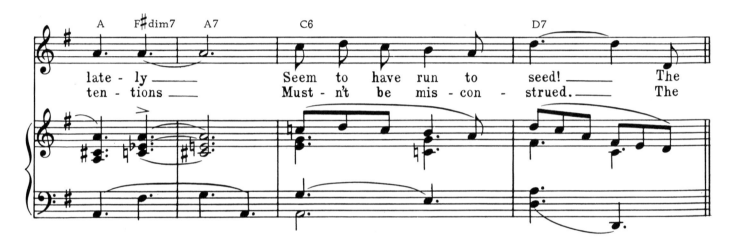

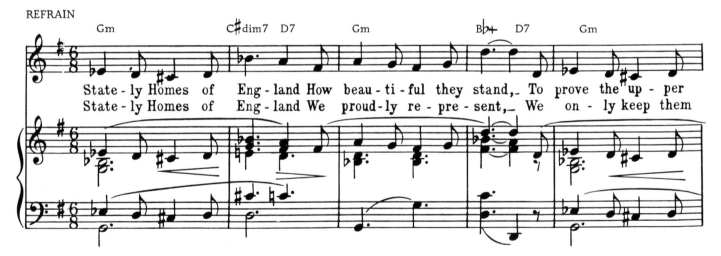

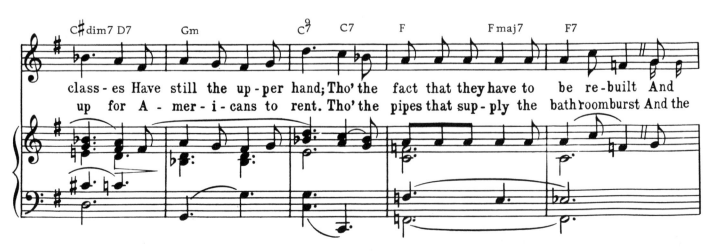

102

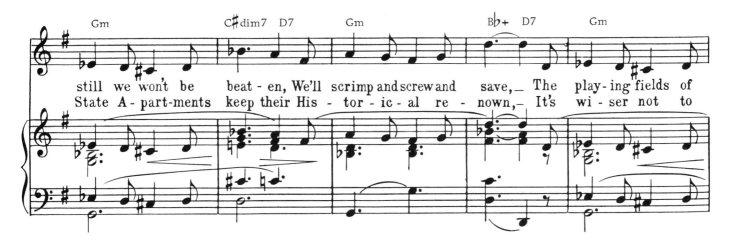

Nun _____ Who re - sent - ed it, And peo-ple who come to call Meet her in the

hall._ The ba-by in the guest wing Who crouch-es by the grate,_ Was wall'd up in the

west wing In Four-teen Twen-ty - Eight._ If a - ny-one spots The Queen of Scots In a

hand em-broid-er'd shroud, We're proud of the State-ly Homes of Eng - land._

We Must All Be Very Kind To
Auntie Jessie

Noël Coward

I remember clearly when a ti-ny lit-tle child My Aunt-ie came to stay with us

May-be as a fam-i-ly we were a tri-fle wild Our spir-its ran a-way with us

Ev-'ry sin-gle day When we were at play Mother used to creep in-to the nur-se-ry and say

We must all be ve-ry kind to Auntie Jes-sie, For she's never been a Mother or a Wife. You mustn't throw your toys at her Or make a vulgar noise at her She hasn't led a ve-ry hap-py life. You must

nev-er lock her playfully in the Bath-room Or play tunes on her enammeled Spanish comb. Tho' un-

-pleasant to be-hold She's a heart of purest gold And Chari-ty you know begins at home. We must home.

Rel - a - tives who come to stay are gen-'ral - ly in-clined To fray the child - ren's

nerves a bit   Something in a maid-en aunt just stup-i-fies the mind   From

Vir - tue's path one swerves a bit   Tho' our child-ish joys

May have made a noise   Moth-er used to mur-mur tho' I *know* Boys will be Boys

OPERETTE (1938), Kenneth Carten, Ross Landon, John Gattrell, and Hugh French sing "The Stately Homes Of England"

TONIGHT AT 8:30, Noël Coward and Gertrude Lawrence perform "Has Anybody Seen Our Ship?" (1936)

Right, Bea Lillie and Richard Haydn in SET TO MUSIC (1939)

BEA LILLIE sings "I Went To A Marvelous Party" from "Set To Music" (1939)

I Went To A Marvelous Party

"SET TO MUSIC"

Noël Coward

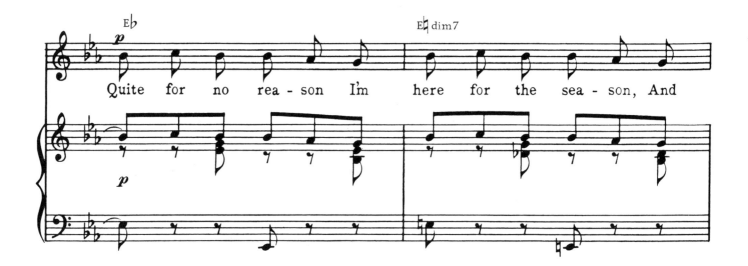

Quite for no rea-son I'm here for the sea-son, And

high as a kite. Liv-ing in er-ror With

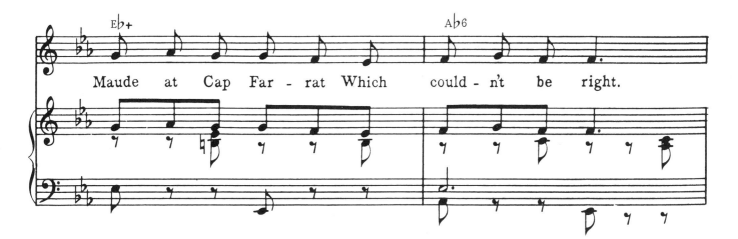

Maude at Cap Far - rat Which could - n't be right.

Ev - 'ry - one's here and fright - f'lly gay,

No - bod - y cares what peo - ple say, Tho' the Ri - vie - ra Seems

real - ly much queer - er Than Rome at its height. Yes - ter - day night --

shells and a black feath-er boa.___ Poor Mill-i-cent wore a sur-

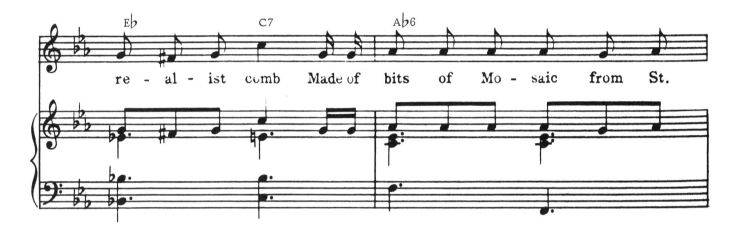

re-al-ist comb Made of bits of Mo-saic from St.

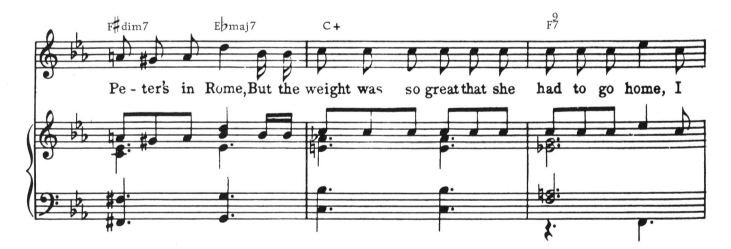

Pe-ter's in Rome, But the weight was so great that she had to go home, I

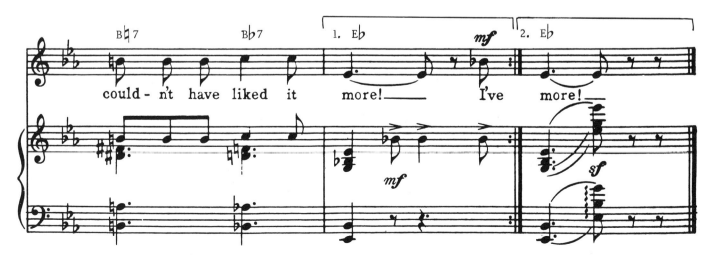

could-n't have liked it more!___ I've more!___

Three White Feathers

"SET TO MUSIC"

NOËL COWARD

I can't help feel - ing Fate's made a fool of me
By eas - y sta - ges Though my be - gin - nings were

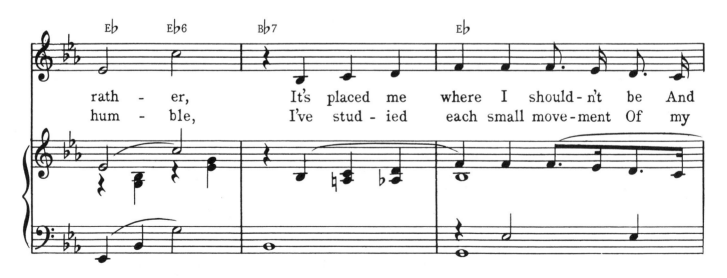

rath - er, It's placed me where I should - n't be And
hum - ble, I've stud - ied each small move - ment Of my

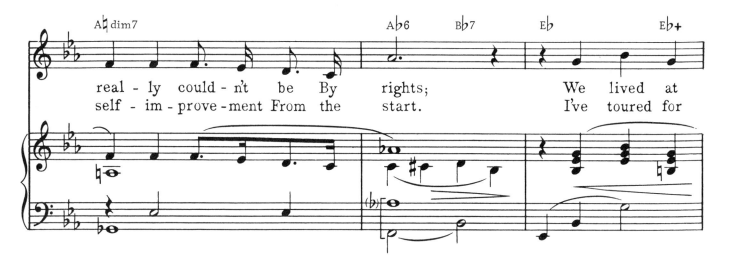

real - ly could - n't be By rights;   We lived at
self - im - prove - ment From the start.   I've toured for

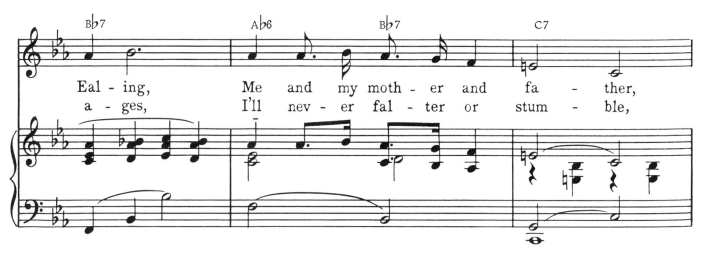

Eal - ing,   Me and my moth - er and fa - ther,
a - ges,   I'll nev - er fal - ter or stum - ble,

I've scaled the so - cial lad - der And I've nev - er had a Head for
I'll give an air of breed - ing And a first-rate read - ing Of the

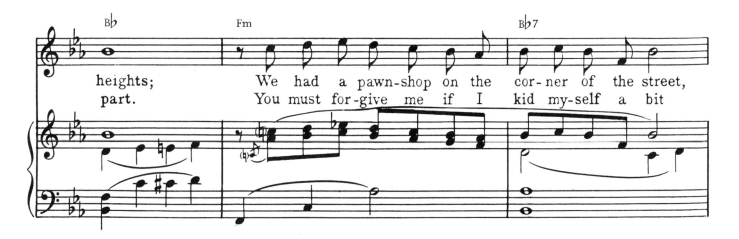

heights;   We had a pawn-shop on the cor - ner of the street,
part.   You must for-give me if I kid my-self a bit

118

And fa-ther did a roar-ing trade,
In this ti - a - ra and this gown.
I used to think those rings and
And tho' my ac - cent may not

neck-lac-es were sweet,
al - to-geth-er fit,
Now I would-n't give them to my maid.
Don't be a-fraid I'll let you down.

REFRAIN

I've trav-ell'd a long, long way And the journ-ey has-n't been all
I've trav-ell'd a long, long way And— had a lot of jolts and

jam, I must ad - mit The Rolls in which I sit Is
bumps; I'll con - cen-trate And be a-head of fate Which—

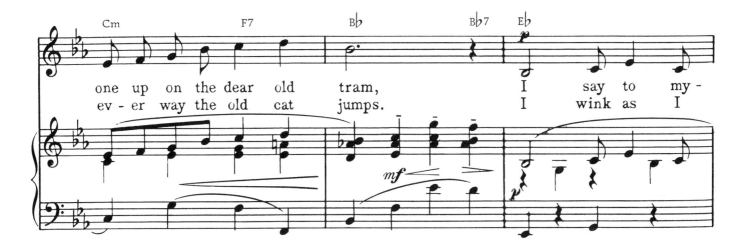

one up on the dear old tram,
ev - er way the old cat jumps.

I say to my -
I wink as I

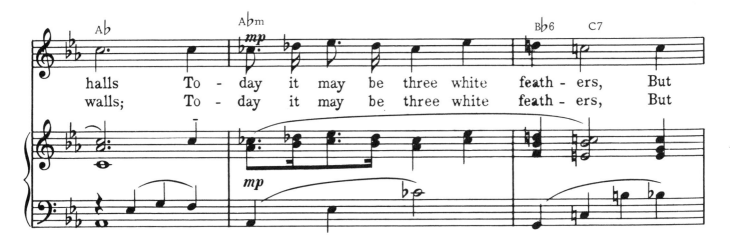

self each day In def - in - ite - ly mar - ble
sly - ly drink To the an - ces - tors that line our

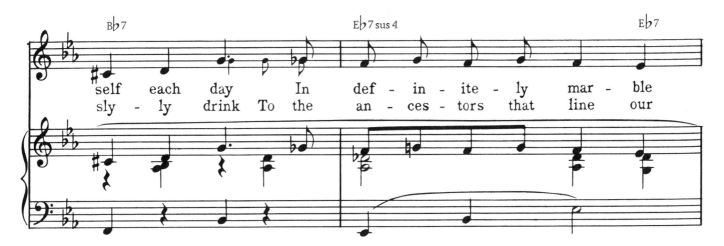

halls To - day it may be three white feath - ers, But
walls; To - day it may be three white feath - ers, But

yes - ter - day it was three brass balls.
yes - ter - day it was three brass balls.

London Pride

Noël Coward

1. Lon-don Pride has been hand-ed down to us, Lon-don Pride is a flow-er that's free.
2. Lon-don Pride has been hand-ed down to us, Lon-don Pride is a flow-er that's free.

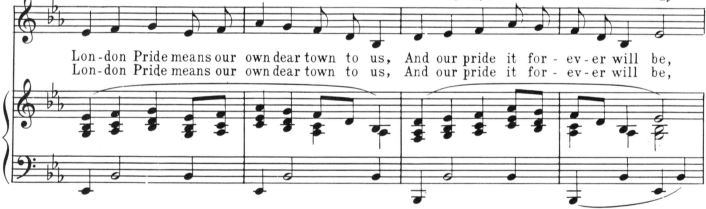

Lon-don Pride means our own dear town to us, And our pride it for-ev-er will be,
Lon-don Pride means our own dear town to us, And our pride it for-ev-er will be,

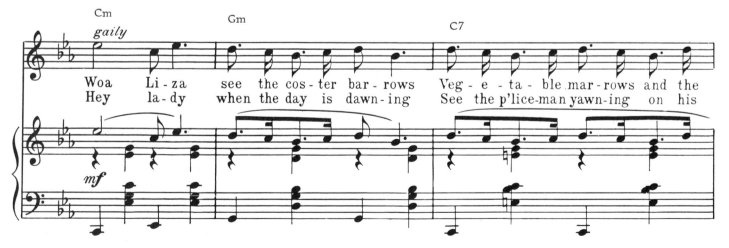

Woa Li - za see the cos-ter bar-rows Veg-e-ta-ble mar-rows and the
Hey la - dy when the day is dawn-ing See the p'lice-man yawn-ing on his

121

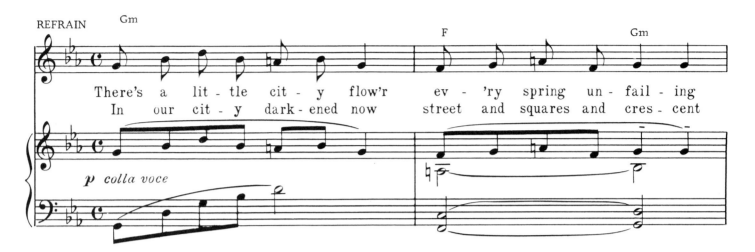

There's a lit-tle cit-y flow'r ev-'ry spring un-fail-ing
In our cit-y dark-ened now street and squares and cres-cent

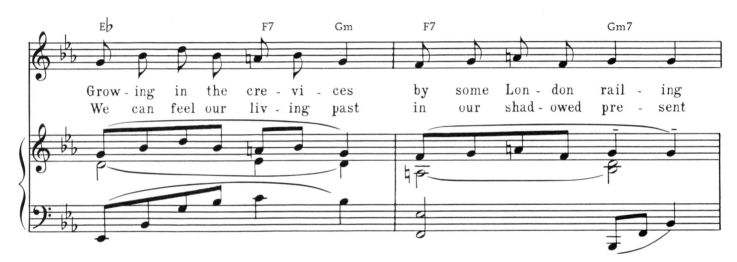

Grow-ing in the cre-vi-ces by some Lon-don rail-ing
We can feel our liv-ing past in our shad-owed pre-sent

Tho' it has a Lat-in name in town and coun-try side
Ghosts be-side our star-lit Thames who lived and loved and died

We in Eng-land call it Lon-don Pride.
Keep through-out the a-ges Lon-don Pride.

Dal Segno

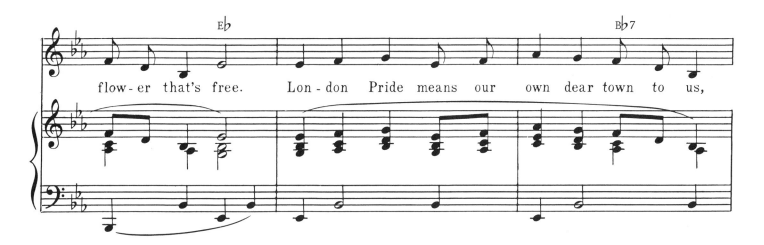

3. Lon - don Pride has been hand - ed down to us, Lon - don Pride is a flow - er that's free. Lon - don Pride means our own dear town to us,

And our pride it for - ev - er will be, Grey, cit - y

stub - born - ly im - plant - ed Tak - en so for grant - ed for a thou - sand years.

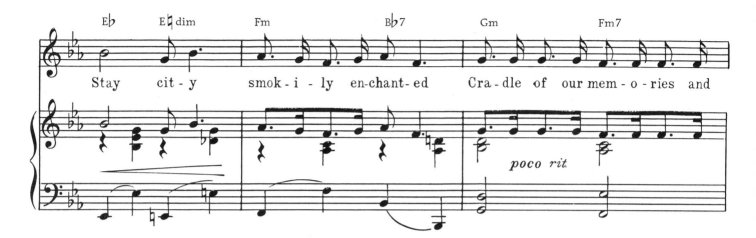

Matelot

"SIGH NO MORE"

Noël Coward

126

Nina

"SIGH NO MORE"

Noël Coward

131

132

133

dance!

CODA

There surely never could have been a__ More ir-rit-at-ing girl than Ni - na__

They never speak in Ar-gen - ti - na__ Of this de-gen-er-ate 'Bam-bi - na'__

rit. Who had the luck to find ro - mance *a tempo* And res-o-lute-ly wouldn't da - -

- - - - - - - nce! She wouldn't dance!- Hola!! *Spoken*

This Is A Changing World

"PACIFIC 1860"

Noël Coward

The world was young So man-y, man-y years a-go ____ The passage of time must show ____

____ Some trac-es of change. Love songs once sung Much laughter, man-y tears Have

ech-oed down the years, The past is old and strange. ____ Each wan-ing

139

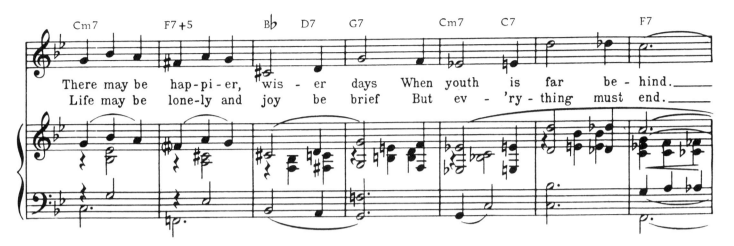

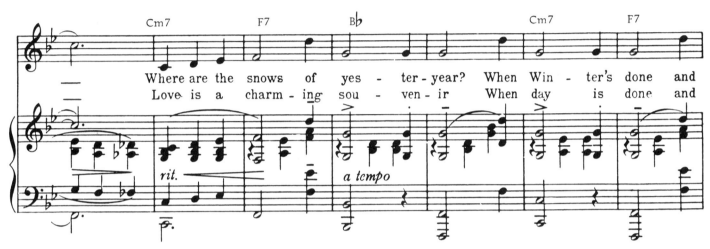

Chase Me, Charlie

"ACE OF CLUBS"

Noël Coward

1. When it's late ____ and the world is sleep - ing,
2. Ev - 'ry night at a - bout e - lev - en,

Our lit - tle black cat, No big - ger than that,
Our lit - tle cat knows, Our lit - tle cat goes,

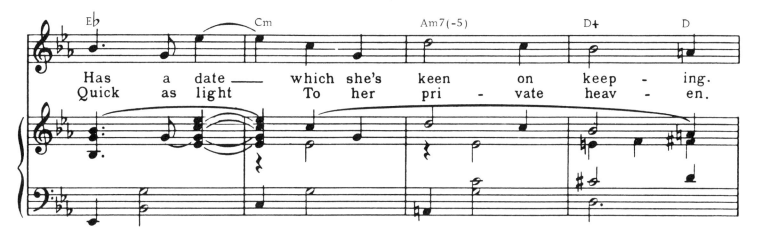

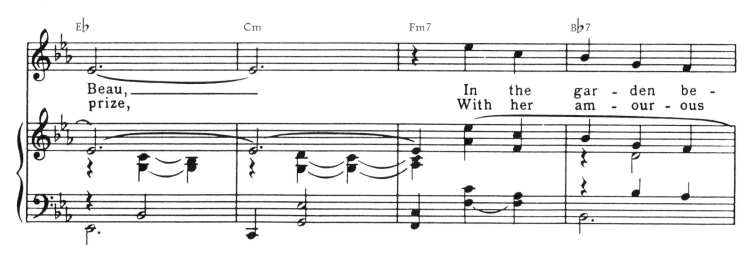

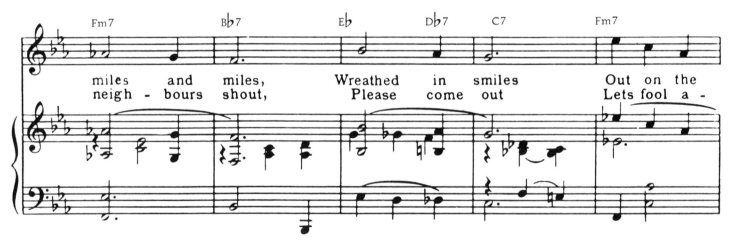

don't be a - fraid to fall,_____ Love in the moon-light can
I'll be your all in all,_____ If you'll ap - pear and be

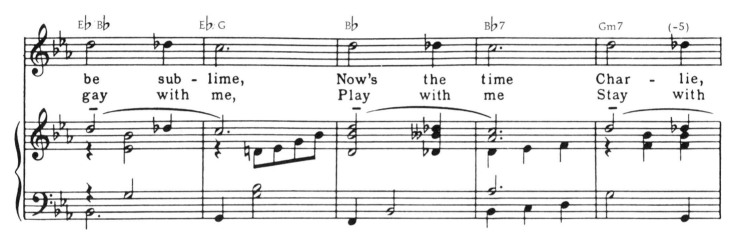

be sub - lime, Now's the time Char - lie,
gay with me, Play with me Stay with

I'm wait-ing for you if you'll on - ly climb,
me? A - ny sug - ges-tions o - kay with me,

O - ver the gar - den wall.
O - ver the gar - den wall._____

144

This is my fi - nal call, _____ Pus - sy - cat,

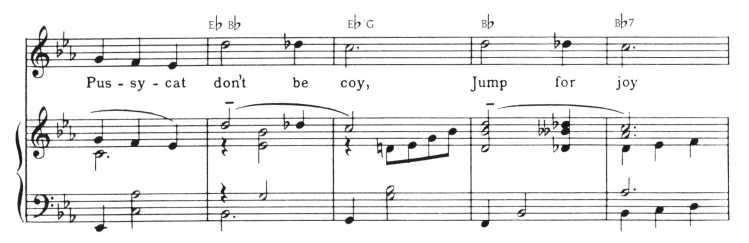

Pus - sy - cat don't be coy, Jump for joy

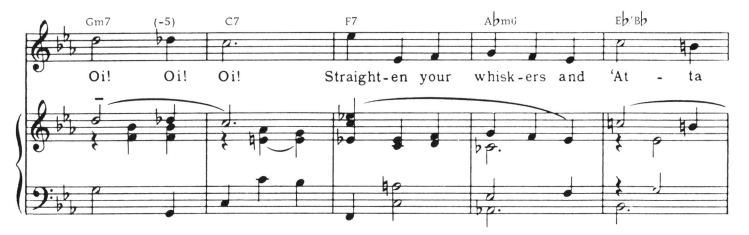

Oi! Oi! Oi! Straight-en your whisk-ers and 'At - ta

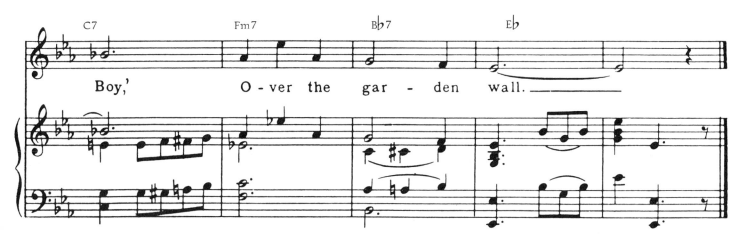

Boy,' O - ver the gar - den wall._____

Above, Night Club Scene from ACE OF CLUBS (1950)

At right, SIGH NO MORE (1945) with Madge Elliott and Cyril Ritchard

Below, Elaine Stritch demonstrates The Little Ones' ABC in SAIL AWAY (1961)

Sail Away

"SAIL AWAY"

NOËL COWARD

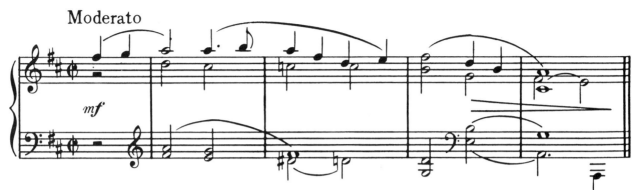

A dif - f'rent sky, New worlds to gaze up - on,

The strange ex - cite - ment of an un - fa - mil - iar shore.

One more good - bye, One more il - lu - sion gone,

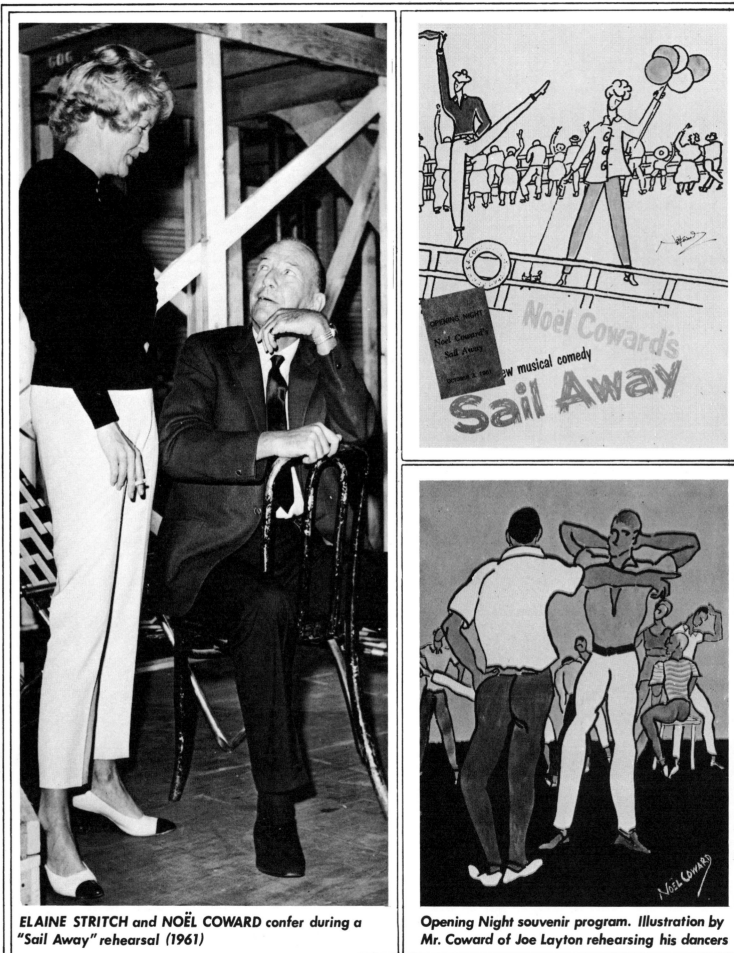

ELAINE STRITCH and **NOËL COWARD** confer during a "Sail Away" rehearsal (1961)

Opening Night souvenir program. Illustration by Mr. Coward of Joe Layton rehearsing his dancers

Something Very Strange

"SAIL AWAY"

NOËL COWARD

Moderato

This is not a day like an - y oth - er day,

This is some-thing spe-cial and a - part. Some-thing to re - mem-ber when the

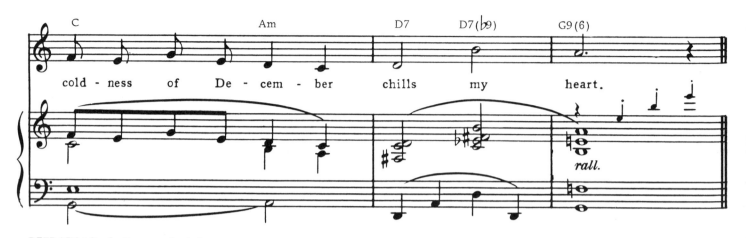

coldness of December chills my heart.

REFRAIN (slowly & expressively)

Something ver-y strange is hap-pen-ing to me. Ev-'ry face I see seems to be
Something ver-y strange is hap-pen-ing to me. Ev-'ry cat I see seems to be

smil - ing. All the sounds I hear, The bus - es chang-ing gear
pur - ring. I can clear-ly tell In ev-'ry clang-ing bell

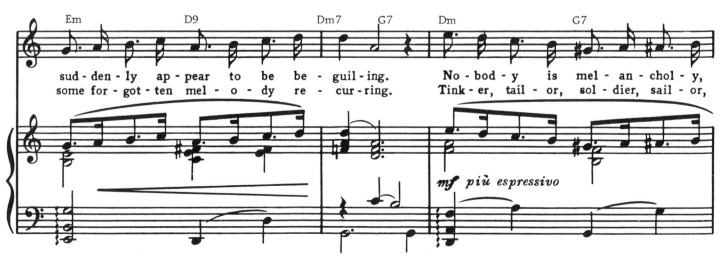

sud - den - ly ap - pear to be be - guil-ing. No-bod-y is mel - an - chol - y,
some for - got-ten mel - o - dy re - cur-ring. Tink - er, tail - or, sol - dier, sail - or,

ELAINE STRITCH in "Sail Away"

Why Do The Wrong People Travel?

"SAIL AWAY"

NOËL COWARD

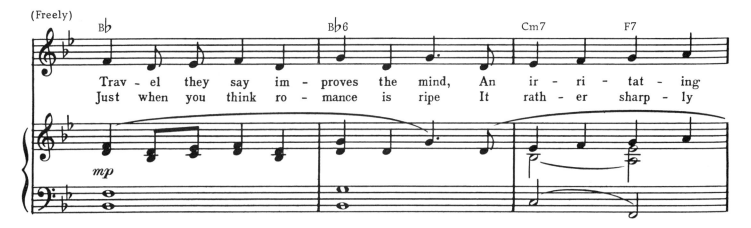

Trav - el they say im - proves the mind, An ir - ri - tat - ing
Just when you think ro - mance is ripe It rath - er sharp - ly

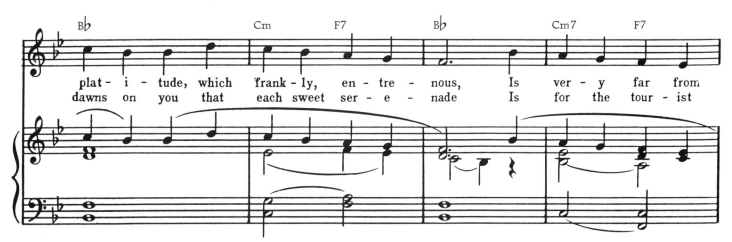

plat - i - tude, which frank - ly, en - tre - nous, Is ver - y far from
dawns on you that each sweet ser - e - nade Is for the tour - ist

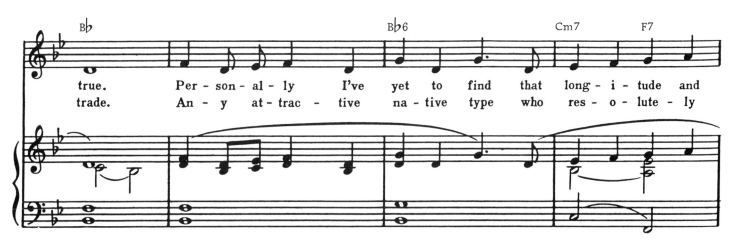

true. Per - son - al - ly I've yet to find that long - i - tude and
trade. An - y at - trac - tive na - tive type who res - o - lute - ly

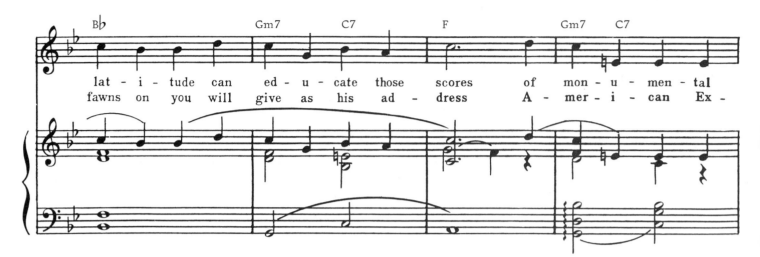

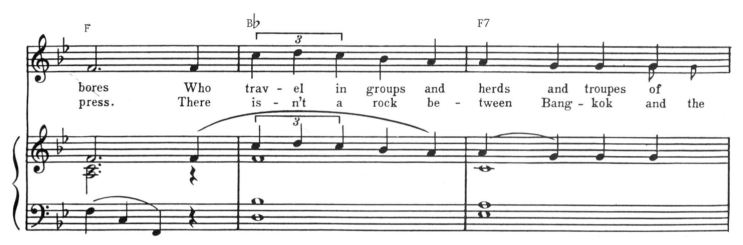

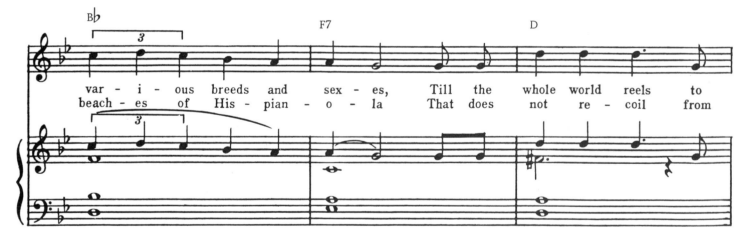

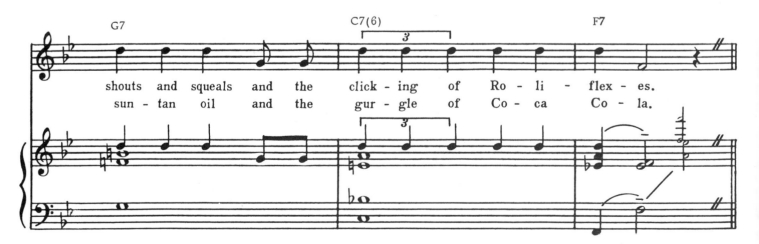

157

FLORENCE HENDERSON and **JOSE FERRER** in "The Girl Who Came To Supper"

Here And Now

"THE GIRL WHO CAME TO SUPPER"

Noël Coward

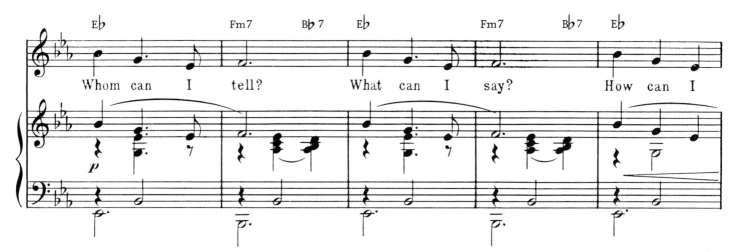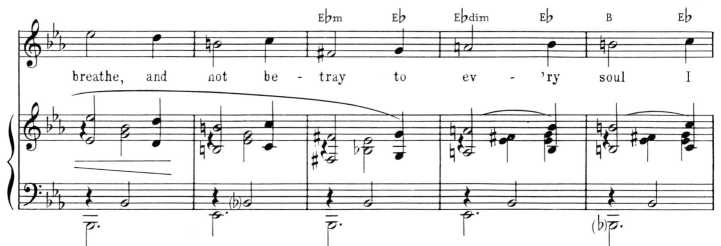

no - bod - y knows. Here and now

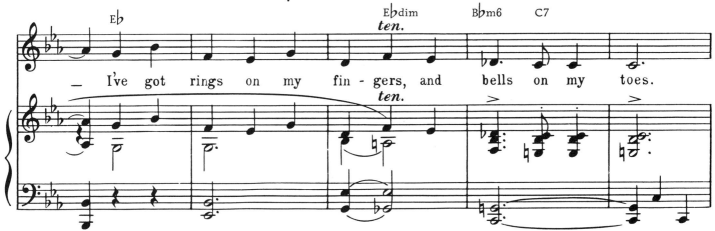

I've got rings on my fin - gers, and bells on my toes.

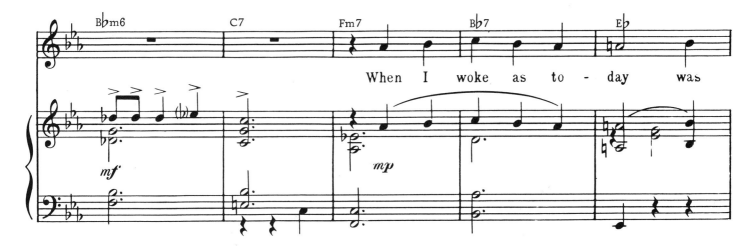

When I woke as to - day was

dawn - ing, All the world seemed to glow.

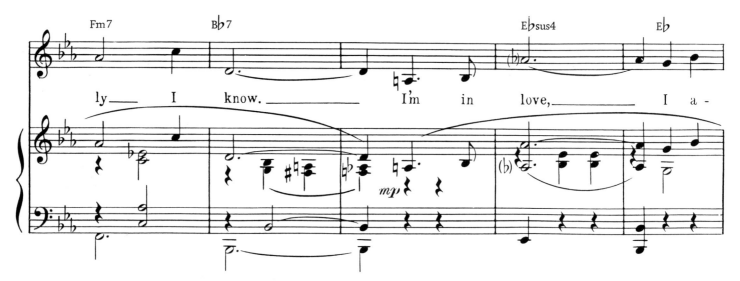

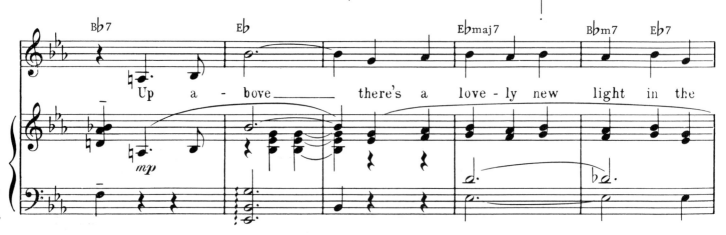

sky._____ When my prince ap - pears, I'll

burst in - to tears and curt - sy three times and bow._____

Who could for - see that such hap-pi - ness could hap-pen to

me here and now? Here and now?_____

London (Is A Little Bit Of All Right)

"THE GIRL WHO CAME TO SUPPER"

NOËL COWARD

Moderato

I was born and bred in Lon - don, It's the on - ly cit - y I

know. Tho' it's fog - gy and cold and wet, I'd be

"The Girl Who Came To Supper" (1963) Top, TESSIE O'SHEA sings "London". Below, Coronation scene.

NOËL COWARD and GERTRUDE LAWRENCE, a team "born to amuse"

Index Of Songs